THE ONE YEAR RETIREMENT DEVOTIONAL FOR WOMEN

5-MINUTE DEVOTIONS TO FIND PURPOSE, GAIN FULFILLMENT, & STRENGTHEN RELATIONSHIPS AS YOU GRACEFULLY TRANSITION INTO THIS NEW CHAPTER OF LIFE

BIBLICAL TEACHINGS

CONTENTS

BIBLE STUDY
-Starter Kit-

Discover a **<u>Simple</u>**, **<u>Powerful</u>** Way to Study
<u>The Bible</u>

- *No More Guesswork* - Learn to Explore the Bible **with Confidence** and Clarity.

- Discover a Study Method That *Fits Seamlessly into Your Busy Life* - **Without the Overwhelm**.

- **Build a Bible Study Routine** *You'll Actually Look Forward To* - Not Just Another Task on Your To-Do List.

<u>SCAN THE QR CODE</u> FOR YOUR <u>FREE</u> COPY

AND SO, THE JOURNEY BEGINS...

SCAN ME

Welcome to "*The One-Year Retirement Devotional for Women*". Retirement is a significant milestone, a transition into a new chapter of life filled with potential and opportunity. Whether you have recently retired or are about to embark on this journey, this devotional is designed to guide you through the changes and challenges you may face.

Within these pages, you'll find 52 weekly devotions, each thoughtfully created to help you discover new purpose, gain fulfillment, and build meaningful connections. The devotions are rooted in scripture and enriched with real-life stories and practical advice, tailored to the unique experiences and needs of retired women.

We understand that retirement brings a mix of emotions—excitement, uncertainty, and perhaps a bit of apprehension. This devotional aims to provide spiritual comfort and practical insights to help you embrace your retirement with grace and joy. Each week, you'll find encouragement to reflect on your past, celebrate your present, and look forward to the future with hope and anticipation.

How to Use This Book:

1. **Weekly Commitment:** Set aside time each week to read a devotion. You can read them in order or pick the one that speaks to you most at any given time. Feel free to date each entry to keep track of your journey. Don't worry if you miss a week— God's guidance is always available.

2. **Begin with Scripture:** Start by reading the title and the relevant Bible verse to set the context for your reflection.

3. **Engage with the Story:** Dive into the narrative and let yourself connect with the experiences shared. These stories are designed to resonate with your own journey.

4. **Reflect and Relate:** After the story, take a moment to reflect on the lessons learned and how they apply to your life. This section is meant to bridge the story with your personal experiences as a retired woman.

5. **Take Action:** Each devotion includes practical action steps. Use these to implement changes and make the lessons a part of your daily life.

6. **Prayer Time:** End your session with the provided prayer, opening your heart to God and seeking His guidance and strength for the week ahead.

As you explore these devotions, you'll encounter themes of faith, courage, love, and new beginnings. From finding new purpose and fulfillment to strengthening relationships and embracing change, each devotion offers valuable insights to enrich your retirement years.

This is YOUR time to grow, to connect, and to thrive. May these devotions become a source of comfort, inspiration, and growth as you transition into this beautiful new chapter. Remember, God's love for you is unwavering, and His plans for you are filled with hope and a future.

Take the first step today. Open your heart, embrace the journey, and let's walk this path together over the next year. Your most fulfilling chapter is just beginning...

Welcome to your journey of retirement.

P.S. *All scripture quotations are taken from the Holy Bible, New International Version (NIV), unless otherwise noted.*

Transitioning Into Retirement

1

THE LAST DAY

___ / ___ / _____

*"For I know the plans I have for you," declares the Lord, "plans
to prosper you and not to harm you, plans to give you hope
and a future."*

— JEREMIAH 29:11

*H*ave you ever felt lost after leaving behind something that
defined you for so many years? The end of my career was
a time of mixed emotions—relief, sadness, and uncertainty all at once. I
remember waking up the first Monday of my retirement, feeling a void
where my routine used to be. As I sipped my morning coffee, I pondered,
"What now?"

Jeremiah 29:11 offers us a profound reassurance during such times of
transition. God's plan for us extends beyond our careers. It encompasses
our entire lives, promising hope and a future filled with purpose.
Embracing this truth helped me see retirement not as an end, but as a
new beginning.

I began to see my days as blank canvases, ready to be painted with new
experiences, passions, and ways to serve. I joined a local volunteer

group, reignited my passion for painting, and spent quality time with family. Each day, I discovered that God's plans for me were still unfolding, filled with opportunities to grow and bless others.

Remember, retirement is not the end of your story. It's a new chapter, written by the Author of Life, who has crafted each page with care and purpose. Embrace this change with an open heart, trusting that God's plans for you are good.

Next Steps

Reflect on a passion or hobby you've set aside. This week, dedicate time to rediscover it. Join a group or take a class related to it, and observe how it enriches your life.

Prayer

Dear God, help me to embrace this new season of life with hope and trust in Your plans. Guide me to discover new joys and purposes. Amen.

2

REDEFINING ME

___ / ___ / _____

"Therefore, if anyone is in Christ, the new creation has come:
The old has gone, the new is here!"

— 2 CORINTHIANS 5:17

*H*ave you ever woken up one morning, looked in the mirror, and wondered, *"Who am I now?"* Retirement can often bring this question to the forefront as we step away from careers that once defined us. For years, our identities might have been closely tied to our job titles, responsibilities, and professional achievements. But now, in this new season of life, we are called to rediscover and redefine ourselves in the light of God's truth.

2 Corinthians 5:17 reminds us that in Christ, we are new creations. This means that our worth and identity are not anchored in what we do, but in who we are as beloved children of God. This shift can feel disorienting at first, but it is also an opportunity to explore and embrace the fullness of who God created us to be.

Consider this: your career was a chapter, not the entire book of your life. This new chapter is filled with blank pages waiting to be written with new adventures, passions, and purposes. Take this time to explore interests you may have set aside, deepen your relationships, and invest in your spiritual growth. Remember, God is with you in this journey of self-discovery, guiding and shaping you every step of the way.

I knew a woman named Susan. She was a dedicated teacher for over thirty years. Upon retiring, she felt lost without her students and daily routines. But as she leaned into her faith, she discovered a love for painting and joined a local art class. She also started mentoring young women in her church, finding joy in sharing her wisdom and experiences. Susan's story is a beautiful example of how retirement can be a time of rich, fulfilling growth when we allow God to redefine us.

So, take heart. Embrace this new chapter with courage and curiosity. Trust that your identity in Christ is more profound and enduring than any job title. Allow yourself to dream, explore, and grow in ways you never imagined. God has incredible plans for you in this season and beyond.

Next Steps

This week, set aside time each day to reflect on a hobby or interest you've always wanted to pursue. Take the first step towards it—whether that's researching, signing up for a class, or simply setting aside time to practice it.

Prayer

Dear God, help me to embrace my new identity in You and guide me as I explore new passions and purposes in this season. Amen.

3

NEW BEGINNINGS

___ / ___ / _____

"Be strong and courageous. Do not be afraid; do not be discour-
aged, for the Lord your God will be with you wherever
you go."

— JOSHUA 1:9

*H*ave you ever faced a season of change and felt
overwhelmed by uncertainty? Retirement often brings
such a time, when the familiar routines of work life fade away and a new,
uncharted path lies ahead. Yet, it's in these moments that God's promise
in Joshua 1:9 becomes a beacon of hope and assurance.

Margaret, who had dedicated over forty years to her career as a nurse,
felt a profound sense of loss and apprehension when it was time for her
to retire. The hospital, her colleagues, and her patients had been central
to her identity for so long. How would she find purpose and peace in this
new chapter of her life?

Determined to embrace this change with faith, Margaret chose to be
strong and courageous, trusting that God was with her in this transition.
She started by reconnecting with her love for gardening, a hobby she

had neglected due to her demanding job. Every morning, she found solace and joy in tending to her flowers and vegetables, watching them grow and flourish under her care.

As Margaret nurtured her garden, she realized that she was also nurturing her spirit. The peace she found in those quiet moments in her garden spread to other areas of her life. She began volunteering at a local community garden, sharing her knowledge and passion with others. This not only gave her a new sense of purpose but also connected her with a new community.

Margaret's journey shows us that new beginnings, while challenging, can be filled with peace and purpose when we trust in God's presence and embrace the opportunities before us. Retirement is not an end but a new start, a chance to explore passions, build new relationships, and grow spiritually.

Dear reader, like Margaret, you too can find peace in change by leaning into your faith and exploring the interests and activities that bring you joy. Remember, God is with you in every step of this journey, guiding and supporting you.

Next Steps

This week, take a moment to reflect on an activity or hobby you once loved but have set aside. Dedicate time to re-engage with it and observe how it brings peace and fulfillment to your life.

Prayer

Dear God, help me find peace in this new chapter of my life. Guide me to embrace new beginnings with courage and joy. Amen.

4

FACING THE UNKNOWN

___ / ___ / _____

*"Do not be anxious about anything, but in every situation, by
prayer and petition, with thanksgiving, present your
requests to God."*

— PHILIPPIANS 4:6

*H*ave you ever lain awake at night, your mind swirling with worries about the future? Retirement can bring a flood of anxieties and uncertainties. Without the familiar routines and structures of work life, it's easy to feel lost and overwhelmed. But God's word in Philippians 4:6 offers us a powerful antidote to our fears: prayer and thanksgiving.

In those moments of anxiety, it's important to remember that we are not alone. God is with us, ready to hear our concerns and provide comfort. When I first retired, I felt a profound sense of uncertainty. Questions about my purpose, my finances, and my health loomed large. But each time I felt overwhelmed, I turned to prayer, laying my worries before God and thanking Him for His steadfast presence in my life.

Prayer became my anchor. Through it, I found a sense of peace that surpassed my understanding. I started a gratitude journal, writing down at least three things I was thankful for each day. This simple practice shifted my focus from what I lacked to what I had, filling my heart with gratitude and easing my anxiety.

Dear reader, as you navigate this new season, know that it's normal to feel anxious about the unknown. But also know that you have a powerful tool in prayer. Take your worries to God, thank Him for His blessings, and trust in His plan for your future. Remember, God's promise of peace is not contingent on our circumstances but on His unwavering presence in our lives.

Facing the unknown can be daunting, but with God by your side, you can handle it with grace and faith. Embrace this time as an opportunity to deepen your relationship with Him, to lean into His promises, and to grow in your faith. Trust that He has a plan for you, one that is filled with hope and a future.

Next Steps

Start a gratitude journal this week. Each day, write down three things you are thankful for and spend a few minutes in prayer, presenting your concerns to God and thanking Him for His blessings.

Prayer

Dear God, help me to trust in Your plan and find peace in Your presence. Guide me through my anxieties and fill my heart with gratitude. Amen.

5

FINDING JOY AGAIN

___ / ___ / _____

*"For I will turn their mourning into joy and will comfort them
and give them joy for their sorrow."*

— JEREMIAH 31:13

etirement brings with it a whirlwind of emotions. The initial excitement can sometimes be overshadowed by a sense of loss or uncertainty about what lies ahead. However, each ending paves the way for a new beginning, and with it, the opportunity to rediscover joy in unexpected places. Jeremiah 31:13 offers a beautiful promise: God will turn our mourning into joy and comfort us, replacing our sorrow with gladness.

When my friend Alice retired, she initially felt a deep sense of loss. Her career had been a significant part of her identity, and she struggled to find her footing in this new phase of life. But Alice decided not to dwell in her sorrow. She saw retirement as a chance to explore new interests and reconnect with old ones.

Alice had always loved music but had put it aside due to her busy schedule. With more free time on her hands, she joined a local choir. Singing with others brought her immense joy and a renewed sense of purpose. The camaraderie and shared passion within the choir lifted her spirits and filled her days with happiness. She also began volunteering at a community center, using her organizational skills to help with events and programs. Alice found that giving back to the community enriched her life in ways she hadn't anticipated.

Alice's story is a testament to the transformative power of embracing new beginnings. By stepping out of her comfort zone and trying new activities, she not only found joy but also built a supportive community around her. Her experience reminds us that it's never too late to find joy again and celebrate the opportunities that new beginnings bring.

Dear reader, as you navigate this new chapter, remember that joy is not a distant memory but a promise from God. Embrace the new beginnings in your life with an open heart, and you will find joy and comfort in unexpected places. Trust that God is with you, turning your mourning into joy and filling your days with His blessings.

Next Steps

This week, identify an activity or interest that you have always wanted to pursue. Take the first step towards it, whether that's signing up for a class, joining a group, or volunteering. Notice how this new beginning brings joy to your life.

Prayer

Dear God, thank You for the promise of joy and new beginnings. Help me to embrace this season with an open heart and find joy in each new day. Amen.

6

FAITH OVER FEAR

___ / ___ / _____

"For I know the plans I have for you," declares the Lord, "plans
to prosper you and not to harm you, plans to give you hope
and a future."

— JEREMIAH 29:11

*D*id you know that nearly 40% of retirees report feeling anxious about their future? It's not uncommon to feel fear when facing the unknown. The transition into retirement can be daunting, but it's also an opportunity to deepen our faith and trust in God's plan for us. Jeremiah 29:11 offers a comforting reminder that God's plans are designed to prosper us and provide hope.

Consider the story of Helen, who had a thriving career as a school principal. When it was time to retire, she felt a mix of excitement and fear. What would she do without the daily structure and purpose her job provided? Helen struggled with uncertainty about her new role and future.

Instead of letting fear control her, Helen turned to her faith. She spent time in prayer, asking God for guidance and peace. She also immersed herself in scripture, finding reassurance in God's promises. Gradually, Helen felt a shift. Her fear began to dissipate, replaced by a growing sense of trust in God's plan for her life.

Helen decided to volunteer at a local literacy program, helping adults learn to read. This new role brought her immense joy and fulfillment. She realized that her skills and passions could still make a significant impact, just in a different context. By trusting God, Helen discovered a new purpose that was equally rewarding.

Helen's experience teaches us that faith can transform our fears into opportunities for growth and joy. Trusting in God's plan doesn't eliminate uncertainty, but it does give us the strength to face it with confidence and hope. When we lean on our faith, we can navigate the unknown with grace, knowing that God's plans are always for our good.

Remember that God's plan for you is filled with hope and promise. Embrace this season with faith, trusting that God will lead you to new and fulfilling opportunities. Let go of fear and hold on to His promises.

Next Steps

This week, spend time each day reflecting on Jeremiah 29:11. Write down any fears or uncertainties you have about the future and pray for God's guidance and peace. Look for ways to serve others using your skills and passions.

Prayer

Dear God, help me to trust in Your plan and let go of my fears. Guide me to new opportunities that bring joy and fulfillment. Amen.

7

CREATING YOUR DAYS

___ / ___ / _____

"Teach us to number our days, that we may gain a heart of wisdom."

— PSALM 90:12

*D*id you know that having a consistent daily routine can significantly improve your mental and emotional well-being? Establishing daily rituals can help bring a sense of purpose and peace to your life, especially during retirement when the structure of a work schedule is no longer present. Psalm 90:12 encourages us to number our days wisely, highlighting the importance of making each day count.

Let me introduce you to Joan, a retired dance teacher. She found herself struggling with the sudden expanse of unstructured time. Without her dance classes and students to fill her days, Joan felt adrift and unproductive. She realized that to thrive in retirement, she needed to create new rhythms that would bring meaning and joy to her daily life.

Joan started by setting a morning ritual. Each day, she began with a cup of tea, followed by a time of prayer and scripture reading. This quiet start grounded her and set a positive tone for the day. She also incorporated a daily walk, which not only kept her physically active but also provided moments of reflection and gratitude.

In the afternoons, Joan dedicated time to learning and creativity. She joined a local book club, took up painting, and even started writing a memoir. These activities stimulated her mind and nurtured her soul. Evening rituals included cooking a healthy dinner and spending quality time with her husband, strengthening their bond.

Joan's daily rituals transformed her retirement experience. By intentionally creating her days, she found a renewed sense of purpose and fulfillment. Her story reminds us that daily rituals, no matter how simple, can bring structure, joy, and spiritual enrichment to our lives.

Try to set up certain daily habits that will bring you joy and connect you with God as you find your way in retirement. Establishing some daily habits can give you a sense of stability and purpose that can turn each day into another meaningful step on this path.

Next Steps

This week, identify one or two rituals you can incorporate into your daily routine. Whether it's a morning prayer, a daily walk, or a creative activity, commit to these practices and observe how they impact your sense of well-being and purpose.

Prayer

Dear God, help me to create daily rituals that honor You and bring joy to my life. Guide me to make each day count in meaningful ways. Amen.

8
LOVING YOURSELF

___ / ___ / _____

"Do you not know that your bodies are temples of the Holy
Spirit, who is in you, whom you have received from God?
You are not your own."

— 1 CORINTHIANS 6:19

*H*ave you ever felt guilty for taking time for yourself? As women, we often prioritize the needs of others over our own, especially during our working years. However, retirement offers a unique opportunity to shift that focus and embrace self-care, recognizing it as an essential part of honoring the temple that God has given us.

In 1 Corinthians 6:19, we are reminded that our bodies are temples of the Holy Spirit. This verse calls us to care for ourselves not out of vanity, but out of reverence for the divine gift of our physical and mental well-being. When I first retired, I struggled with the idea of self-care, feeling that it was selfish to put my needs first. But I soon realized that taking care of myself was not only beneficial for me but also for those around me.

I began to incorporate small acts of self-care into my daily routine. I started my mornings with a peaceful walk, relishing the beauty of nature and the quiet time with God. I found joy in preparing healthy meals, nurturing my body with nutritious foods. I also dedicated time to hobbies that I loved but had neglected, such as reading and painting. These activities revitalized my spirit and brought a renewed sense of joy and fulfillment to my life.

Self-care is not a luxury but a necessity. It's a way to honor God by taking care of the body and mind He has entrusted to you. By prioritizing self-care, you are better equipped to serve others and fulfill the purposes God has for your life. Remember, loving yourself is an integral part of your spiritual journey.

As you embrace this new season, take time to discover what self-care means for you. It could be as simple as enjoying a cup of tea in silence, taking a leisurely bath, or engaging in creative activities that bring you joy. Self-care is deeply personal, and there is no one-size-fits-all approach.

Next Steps

This week, choose one self-care activity that you enjoy and commit to doing it daily. Reflect on how this practice nurtures your spirit and enhances your well-being.

Prayer

Dear God, help me to honor and care for the body and mind You have given me. Teach me to embrace self-care as an act of love and gratitude. Amen.

9

BALANCING LIFE

___ / ___ / _____

"There is a time for everything, and a season for every activity under the heavens."

— ECCLESIASTES 3:1

*N*avigating the freedom that comes with retirement can be both exhilarating and challenging. The absence of a fixed schedule often leaves us wondering how to structure our days in a way that brings balance and fulfillment. Ecclesiastes 3:1 reminds us that there is a time for everything, highlighting the importance of balance and the right season for each activity.

Take the story of Carol, for instance. After decades of a demanding career in corporate finance, Carol suddenly found herself with an abundance of free time and no clear plan on how to fill it. Initially, she enjoyed the leisure, but soon felt restless and unproductive. Realizing that she needed structure, Carol decided to create a schedule that balanced rest, productivity, and enjoyment.

Carol began by prioritizing her spiritual well-being. She started each day with a quiet time of prayer and Bible study, grounding herself in God's word and finding peace for the day ahead. Next, she dedicated specific hours to physical activity, joining a local gym and taking up yoga. This not only improved her health but also boosted her energy levels.

To ensure she stayed mentally active, Carol set aside time for reading and learning new skills, such as cooking and photography. She also made it a point to volunteer at her church twice a week, finding fulfillment in serving others and staying connected with her community.

Through trial and error, Carol discovered a rhythm that worked for her. She found that a balanced schedule brought harmony to her life, enabling her to enjoy the fruits of her labor while also exploring new passions and serving her community. Carol's experience underscores the importance of creating a schedule that respects our need for both activity and rest, productivity and relaxation.

Dear reader, retirement offers you a unique opportunity to craft a life that reflects your values and passions. Take time to find your balance, ensuring that each day includes moments for spiritual growth, physical health, mental stimulation, and community involvement. Trust that God will guide you in creating a harmonious schedule that brings joy and fulfillment.

Next Steps

This week, create a daily schedule that includes time for spiritual activities, physical exercise, mental pursuits, and community service. Adjust as needed until you find a balance that brings harmony to your life.

Prayer

Dear God, help me to find balance in my daily life. Guide me to create a harmonious schedule that nurtures my body, mind, and spirit. Amen.

ADJUSTING THE SAILS

___ / ___ / _____

*The heart of man plans his way, but the Lord establishes his
steps."*

— PROVERBS 16:9 (ESV)

*H*ave you ever found yourself feeling lost when your daily
routine changes? Retirement can bring a sudden shift
from a structured schedule to a more flexible, yet often uncertain, way of
life. This transition is much like sailing; sometimes the winds change,
and we must adjust our sails to stay on course. Proverbs 16:9 reminds us
that while we make our plans, it is the Lord who directs our steps.

When I first retired, I struggled to find a new rhythm. My days, once
filled with meetings and deadlines, now felt wide open and unstructured. It was disorienting, and I felt a bit adrift. However, I soon realized
that this was an opportunity to create a routine that reflected my new
priorities and passions.

I began by identifying what was most important to me in this new
season. I wanted to grow closer to God, maintain my health, and explore
new hobbies. With these goals in mind, I started to structure my days

around them. Morning prayer and Bible study became the cornerstone of my routine, grounding me in God's word and setting a positive tone for the day. I also set aside time for exercise, whether it was a brisk walk or a gentle yoga session, to keep my body healthy and active. Afternoons were often reserved for pursuing hobbies like gardening and painting, activities that brought me joy and fulfillment.

As I adjusted my sails and settled into this new routine, I found a renewed sense of purpose and peace. My days felt balanced and intentional, guided by the priorities I had set and the gentle direction of God's hand.

Adjusting your routine in retirement is an opportunity to align your daily life with what truly matters to you. Take time to reflect on your goals and passions, and be willing to make changes that support your well-being and spiritual growth. Remember, it's okay to experiment and adjust as needed; what's important is finding a rhythm that brings you joy and fulfillment.

Next Steps

This week, take some time to evaluate your current routine. Identify one area that could be improved or adjusted to better align with your goals. Make a small, practical change and observe how it impacts your day.

Prayer

Dear God, guide me as I adjust my daily routine. Help me to create a balanced and fulfilling life that honors You and nurtures my spirit. Amen.

Discovering New Passions

11

REKINDLING OLD FLAMES

___ / ___ / _____

"Whatever you do, work at it with all your heart, as working for the Lord, not for human masters."

— COLOSSIANS 3:23

*D*id you know that engaging in hobbies can significantly improve your mental health and overall well-being? Hobbies not only provide relaxation and joy but also offer a sense of accomplishment and purpose. Colossians 3:23 reminds us to do whatever we do with all our heart, as working for the Lord, highlighting the value of dedicating ourselves wholeheartedly to our passions.

Let me tell you about Carol, a retired accountant who had always loved painting. During her career, her passion for art took a backseat to her demanding job and family responsibilities. When she retired, Carol found herself with the time and space to revisit this old flame.

Initially, Carol felt a bit rusty and unsure about picking up the paintbrush again. But she decided to take a step of faith and signed up for a local art class. With each stroke of the brush, she felt her confidence and joy returning. The act of creating something beautiful brought her immense satisfaction and a renewed sense of purpose.

Carol's rediscovered hobby not only filled her days with joy but also connected her with a community of like-minded individuals. She began participating in local art shows and even sold a few of her pieces. This new chapter in her life was enriched by the passion she had reignited, proving that it's never too late to reconnect with the things we love.

Carol's story is a beautiful reminder that our hobbies and passions are gifts from God, meant to be enjoyed and shared. Whether it's painting, gardening, knitting, or playing an instrument, these activities can bring us closer to God and to others. By dedicating time to our hobbies, we honor the creativity and joy that God has placed within us.

So, why not consider rekindling an old hobby or passion? Allow yourself to enjoy the process, and remember to do it with all your heart, as unto the Lord. You may find that this activity not only fills your days with joy but also brings new opportunities and connections into your life.

Next Steps

This week, take the first step to reconnect with a hobby you once loved. Gather the materials you need and set aside dedicated time to immerse yourself in this activity for at least 30 minutes a day. Notice how it impacts your mood and sense of fulfillment. Consider journaling this each day.

Prayer

Dear God, thank You for the passions and hobbies You have placed in my heart. Help me to reconnect with these joys and honor You through them. Amen.

12

ADVENTUROUS SPIRIT

___ / ___ / _____

"Be strong and courageous. Do not be afraid; do not be discour-
aged, for the Lord your God will be with you wherever
you go."

— JOSHUA 1:9

*H*ave you ever wondered what new adventures await you in this season of life? Retirement is a perfect time to explore new activities and experiences that you never had time for before. Joshua 1:9 encourages us to be strong and courageous, reassuring us that God is with us wherever we go.

When I retired, I found myself with the freedom to step outside my comfort zone and try something new. Encouraged by friends, I decided to join a hiking group, even though I had never been much of an outdoor enthusiast.

At first, I was hesitant and a bit fearful of the unfamiliar terrain. But with each hike, I grew more confident and discovered a new love for nature. The fresh air, the breathtaking views, and the camaraderie with my fellow hikers brought me immense joy and a sense of accomplishment.

This new activity not only enriched me physically but also spiritually, as I often found myself marveling at God's creation and feeling closer to Him.

My adventurous spirit didn't stop there. I went on to try other activities like painting, bird-watching, and even taking a cooking class. Each new experience added a layer of excitement and fulfillment to my life, proving that it's never too late to discover new passions.

My story is a testament to the blessings that come from stepping out of our comfort zones and embracing new adventures. It reminds us that God is with us, guiding and encouraging us as we explore new horizons. By trying new activities, we not only enrich our own lives but also inspire those around us to do the same.

Embrace the spirit of adventure. It might be scary at first but you can trust that God will be with you as you try new activities, and discover new people, places, and passions. Let this be a time of growth, joy, and exploration.

Next Steps

This week, choose one new activity you've always wanted to try. Whether it's joining a club, taking a class, or exploring the outdoors, commit to giving it a go. Reflect on how this new experience impacts your perspective and joy.

Prayer

Dear God, give me the courage to try new activities and embrace the adventures that come my way. Thank You for being with me in every step. Amen.

13

CREATIVE FLOW

___ / ___ / _____

"For we are God's handiwork, created in Christ Jesus to do good works, which God prepared in advance for us to do."

— EPHESIANS 2:10

*H*ave you ever tried your hand at pottery, joined a dance class, or perhaps taken up baking exotic pastries? Retirement is the perfect time to dive into a myriad of creative activities and see what brings you joy. Ephesians 2:10 reminds us that we are God's handiwork, created to do good works, and part of that creation is expressing the unique creativity He has placed within us.

After retiring, you may have felt the freedom to explore new hobbies and interests. Imagine the excitement of trying something completely different each month and discovering hidden talents you never knew you had. This was my experience as I ventured into various creative outlets after retirement.

First, I joined a pottery class. Although my initial pieces were far from perfect, the process of molding clay with my hands was incredibly therapeutic. Next, I decided to learn ballroom dancing. The rhythm of the music and the joy of movement brought a new spark to my life. Then, I took up baking, experimenting with recipes from around the world and sharing the delicious results with friends and family.

Each new activity brought its own set of challenges and rewards, but the common thread was the immense joy and fulfillment I found in the process. Engaging in these creative pursuits allowed me to express myself in new ways and connect with others who shared similar interests. It also provided a deeper sense of purpose and a way to glorify God through the talents He has given me.

Just like my journey, you have the potential to find new creative outlets that can enrich your life. Creativity is a gift from God, and engaging in creative activities can be a form of worship, a way to connect with God and express gratitude for the talents He has given you.

As you explore new creative outlets, remember that it's not about perfection but about the joy and fulfillment you find in the process. Allow yourself the freedom to experiment and make mistakes. Each step you take in your creative journey is a step towards discovering more about yourself and the unique ways God has designed you.

Next Steps

This week, choose one new creative activity you've always wanted to try. Set aside time each day to engage in this activity and reflect on how it makes you feel. Notice the joy and sense of accomplishment that comes from expressing your creativity.

Prayer

Dear God, thank You for the creative talents You have given me. Help me to find joy and fulfillment in new creative outlets. Guide me as I explore and express the creativity You have placed within me. Amen.

14

NEVER CEASE LEARNING

___ / ___ / _____

*"Let the wise hear and increase in learning, and the one who
understands obtain guidance."*

— PROVERBS 1:5 (ESV)

*W*hen was the last time you tried something new just for
the fun of it? Retirement is the perfect time to rediscover
the joy of learning and growing in new directions. Proverbs 1:5 encourages us to be wise by continually increasing our learning and seeking
guidance.

Just like many retirees, Linda, a former marketing executive, found
herself wondering how to fill the void left by her bustling career in the
world of advertising. Linda was looking forward to the slower pace of
retirement but, she soon found herself feeling unchallenged and a bit
bored. Linda realized she needed to engage her mind and continue
growing intellectually and creatively.

Linda decided to enroll in a variety of classes and workshops. She
started with a cooking class, something she had always wanted to try but
never had the time for. The hands-on experience in the kitchen reignited

her passion for food and creativity. Encouraged by this, she signed up for a local history course at the community college, which deepened her appreciation for her hometown and its rich past.

The more Linda learned, the more energized she felt. She joined a book club to explore new genres of literature and participated in a photography workshop, discovering a new way to capture and appreciate the beauty around her. Each new class and workshop brought fresh excitement and purpose to her days.

Linda's experience is a powerful reminder that it's never too late to learn and grow. By engaging in lifelong learning, we not only enrich our own lives but also stay connected to the world around us. Whether it's a formal class or an informal workshop, these learning opportunities can open new doors and spark new passions.

Reflect on your own journey. Are there new skills or subjects you've always wanted to explore? This is the perfect time to try something new and see where it takes you. Embrace the opportunity to learn and grow in this new season of life, just as Linda did.

Next Steps

This week, research local classes or workshops that interest you. Enroll in one that excites you and commit to attending regularly. Reflect on how learning something new brings vitality and joy to your life.

Prayer

Dear God, inspire me to continue growing and learning in this season of my life. Guide me to new opportunities that enrich my mind and spirit. Amen.

15

THE WORLD OF WORDS

___ / ___ / _____

*"Let the word of Christ dwell in you richly, teaching and
admonishing one another in all wisdom, singing psalms
and hymns and spiritual songs, with thankfulness in your
hearts to God."*

— COLOSSIANS 3:16 (ESV)

*H*ave you ever felt the transformative power of a good book
or the therapeutic effect of putting pen to paper? Retirement offers a wonderful opportunity to dive deep into the world of
words, both through reading and writing. Colossians 3:16 encourages us
to let the word of Christ dwell in us richly, reminding us of the profound
impact words can have on our hearts and minds.

When I retired, I finally had the time to indulge in my love for reading. I
joined a local book club, and it quickly became one of my favorite activities. Each month, we read a new book and gathered to discuss it. The
stories we read opened up new worlds and perspectives, enriching my
life in ways I hadn't anticipated. The discussions with fellow book lovers
also deepened my understanding and appreciation of each book.

Inspired by the books I read, I also began to write. I started with journaling, capturing my thoughts and reflections each day. This simple practice became a therapeutic outlet, helping me process my experiences and emotions. Over time, my journaling evolved into writing short stories and memoirs. Writing allowed me to express myself creatively and leave a legacy of words for my family.

Reading and writing have become integral parts of my daily routine, bringing joy, wisdom, and a deeper connection to God's word. Through reading, I immerse myself in stories that broaden my horizons and nurture my spirit. Through writing, I find clarity, creativity, and a sense of purpose.

So, will you answer the call from the world of words? Whether you start by reading a book that interests you or writing your thoughts and stories, you'll find that these activities can enrich your life in profound ways. Let the word of Christ dwell in you richly, and allow the power of words to transform your heart and mind.

Next Steps

This week, choose a book to read that interests you and set aside time each day to enjoy it. Additionally, start a journal and write down your thoughts, reflections, or even a story. Observe how reading and writing bring new joy and insight into your life.

Prayer

Dear God, thank You for the gift of words. Help me to find joy in reading and writing, and let Your word dwell richly in my heart. Amen.

16

TECH-SAVVY

___ / ___ / _____

*"Whatever you do, work at it with all your heart, as working
for the Lord, not for human masters."*

— COLOSSIANS 3:23

*D*id you know that learning new technology can be just as exciting and rewarding as picking up a new hobby? Embracing technology in retirement can open up a world of possibilities, from staying connected with loved ones to discovering new interests and skills. Colossians 3:23 encourages us to do whatever we do with all our heart, and this includes navigating the digital world.

Imagine being able to video call your grandchildren, join online communities of like-minded individuals, or even start a blog to share your life experiences and wisdom. Technology can make all these things possible and more. It's never too late to become tech-savvy, and the benefits are endless.

Consider the story of my friend, Anne. After retiring, Anne felt a bit disconnected from the fast-paced digital world her grandchildren were so comfortable in. Determined to bridge the gap, she decided to take a basic computer course at her local library. She learned how to use email, social media, and even some basic photo editing software.

Anne soon found herself video chatting with her family across the country, sharing photos and stories online, and even joining a virtual book club. The more she learned, the more confident she became. Technology became a tool for her to stay connected, continue learning, and even make new friends.

Just like Anne, you can embrace technology and use it to enhance your retirement. Whether it's learning how to use a smartphone, setting up a social media account, or exploring online classes and workshops, there are countless ways to become tech-savvy.

Dear reader, as you navigate this new season, consider the opportunities that technology can offer. It's a wonderful way to stay engaged, connected, and continually learning. Remember, whatever you do, work at it with all your heart, knowing that you are enriching your life and honoring God with your efforts.

Next Steps

This week, choose one new piece of technology or digital skill you've always wanted to learn. Take the first step by signing up for a class, watching tutorial videos, or asking a friend for help. Reflect on how this new knowledge enhances your life and connections.

Prayer

Dear God, help me to embrace new technologies and use them to stay connected and continue learning. Guide me as I explore these new tools and enrich my life. Amen.

17

HEART OF SERVICE

___ / ___ / _____

*"Each of you should use whatever gift you have received to
serve others, as faithful stewards of God's grace in its
various forms."*

— 1 PETER 4:10

*M*any people find that their happiness and well-being improve significantly when they start volunteering. The act of serving others not only benefits those in need but also brings joy and fulfillment to the giver. 1 Peter 4:10 reminds us to use our unique gifts to serve others, being faithful stewards of God's grace.

Like many retirees, Susan felt a void in her life during post-work life. Used to the daily hustle and the sense of accomplishment from her job, she longed for a way to contribute meaningfully to her community. That's when she decided to explore volunteer opportunities.

Susan started by considering her passions and skills. She loved organizing events and had a heart for helping children. Combining these interests, she volunteered with a local after-school program. Her organizational skills helped streamline the program's activities, and her compassionate nature made her a favorite among the children.

The impact was profound. Not only did the children benefit from her dedication, but Susan also felt a renewed sense of purpose. Her days were filled with meaningful interactions and the joy of making a difference. Volunteering also connected her with like-minded individuals, expanding her social circle and bringing new friendships into her life.

Susan's story highlights the joy and fulfillment that come from serving others. By finding volunteer opportunities that align with our passions and skills, we can experience a deeper sense of purpose and connection in our retirement years. Whether it's mentoring, organizing community events, or simply offering a helping hand, there are countless ways to serve.

How could you use your unique gifts and skills to serve others? Volunteering is not only a way to give back but also a path to discovering new joys and building lasting relationships. Embrace the heart of service and let God guide you to opportunities where you can make a meaningful impact.

Next Steps

This week, identify a cause or organization that resonates with you. Reach out to them and explore how you can volunteer your time and talents. Notice how serving others enriches your life and brings new joy.

Prayer

Dear God, help me to find meaningful ways to serve others. Guide me to volunteer opportunities where I can use my gifts to make a difference. Amen.

18

MAKING A DIFFERENCE

___ / ___ / _____

"You are the light of the world. A town built on a hill cannot be hidden. In the same way, let your light shine before others, that they may see your good deeds and glorify your Father in heaven."

— MATTHEW 5:14,16

*H*ave you ever considered how your actions can ripple out to impact your entire community? Retirement provides a unique opportunity to step into new roles of service and leadership. Matthew 5:14,16 calls us to be the light of the world, letting our good deeds shine brightly for all to see, bringing glory to God.

When I retired, I found myself with a desire to give back to my community in meaningful ways. I started by volunteering at a local food bank, sorting donations and helping distribute food to those in need. The gratitude and relief on the faces of the recipients filled my heart with joy and purpose. I realized that even small acts of kindness can make a significant difference.

Inspired by this experience, I looked for other ways to serve. I joined a community garden project, where I helped plant and maintain a garden that provided fresh produce to local families. Working alongside my neighbors, we built not just a garden but a sense of camaraderie and shared purpose. The garden became a place where people could come together, connect, and support each other.

Through these activities, I discovered the profound impact we can have when we use our time and talents to serve others. It's not always about grand gestures; often, it's the small, consistent acts of kindness that truly light up our communities. Whether it's volunteering, mentoring, or simply being a good neighbor, every action counts.

Dear reader, as you embark on this new chapter of your life, remember that you have the power to make a difference. Look for opportunities to serve and impact your community. Let your light shine brightly, so others may see your good deeds and be inspired to do the same. Together, we can create a ripple effect of kindness and love that glorifies our Father in heaven.

Next Steps

This week, identify a community project or organization that resonates with you. Reach out to see how you can get involved. Whether it's volunteering, donating, or offering your skills, take a step to make a positive impact in your community.

Prayer

Dear God, help me to be a light in my community. Guide me to opportunities where I can make a difference and show Your love through my actions. Amen.

19

LEGACY OF WISDOM

___ / ___ / _____

"The righteous will flourish like a palm tree, they will grow like
a cedar of Lebanon; planted in the house of the Lord, they
will flourish in the courts of our God. They will still bear
fruit in old age, they will stay fresh and green."

— PSALM 92:12-14

*H*ave you ever considered the impact your life experiences can have on others? Research shows that sharing wisdom and knowledge not only benefits the receiver but also provides a deep sense of fulfillment and purpose for the giver. Psalm 92:12-14 reminds us that even in our later years, we are capable of bearing fruit and staying fresh and vibrant.

When Martha retired from her long career as an engineer, she felt a wealth of untapped knowledge and experience that she didn't want to go to waste. Her years of solving complex problems and working on innovative projects had taught her invaluable lessons about perseverance, creativity, and teamwork. Martha realized that her journey could inspire and guide others, so she sought ways to share her wisdom.

Martha began by mentoring young engineering students at a nearby college. She shared not only technical skills but also the importance of critical thinking and collaboration. Her stories and insights resonated deeply with the students, who appreciated her practical advice and heartfelt encouragement.

Additionally, Martha joined a local writing group and started working on her memoirs. Documenting her experiences allowed her to reflect on her life's journey and pass on the lessons she had learned to her family and future generations. Her writing became a cherished project, giving her a renewed sense of purpose and creativity.

Martha's efforts did not go unnoticed. Her mentees often expressed their gratitude, telling her how her guidance had impacted their careers and lives. Her memoirs inspired others to document their own stories, creating a ripple effect of shared wisdom and connection.

There are countless ways to share your wisdom, whether through mentoring, writing, or simply having meaningful conversations with those around you. Your legacy of wisdom can bear fruit and bless others, leaving a lasting impact for generations to come.

Next Steps

This week, think about an area of your life where you have gained significant experience and wisdom. Identify a way to share this knowledge, whether through mentoring, writing, or speaking with others. Observe how this sharing enriches both your life and the lives of those you touch.

Prayer

Dear God, thank You for the wisdom and experiences You have given me. Help me to share these gifts with others, bearing fruit and making a positive impact. Amen.

Strengthening Relationships

2 0

CHERISHED MOMENTS

___ / ___ / _____

"Children are a heritage from the Lord, offspring a reward from him."

— PSALM 127:3

here's a special magic in the laughter of children and the warmth of their hugs. Your newfound free time opens up a treasure trove of opportunities to bask in these simple yet profound joys. Psalm 127:3 reminds us that children are a heritage from the Lord, a reward and blessing that enriches our lives.

One of my fondest memories involves a summer spent with my grandchildren. We decided to start a small vegetable garden in my backyard. None of us were expert gardeners, but that was part of the fun. Together, we picked out seeds, planted them, and watered the garden daily. As we worked side by side, we shared stories, laughed at our mistakes, and celebrated each small sprout that peeked through the soil.

One afternoon, after a particularly heavy rain, we discovered that our garden had flourished almost overnight. The look of wonder and excitement on my grandchildren's faces was priceless. They learned about the miracle of growth and the rewards of patience and care. I realized that these moments were not just about gardening; they were about bonding, teaching, and creating lasting memories together.

These cherished moments became a foundation for deeper relationships with my grandchildren. We continued to find simple, meaningful activities to do together—baking cookies, going on nature walks, or just sitting together and talking about life. Each activity strengthened our bond and left us with memories to treasure.

How can you find and create these cherished moments with your children and grandchildren? It doesn't have to be anything grand or elaborate; often, it's the simplest activities that foster the deepest connections. Remember, these moments are gifts from God, opportunities to share love, wisdom, and joy with the next generations.

Next Steps

This week, plan a simple activity to do with your children or grandchildren. It could be anything from cooking a meal together, going for a walk, or starting a small project. Focus on the time spent together and the conversations you share.

Prayer

Dear God, thank You for the gift of my children and grandchildren. Help me to create cherished moments with them and to build strong, loving relationships. Amen.

21

FAMILY TRADITIONS

___ / ___ / _____

"I am reminded of your sincere faith, which first lived in your grandmother Lois and in your mother Eunice and, I am persuaded, now lives in you also."

— 2 TIMOTHY 1:5

*R*etirement is a beautiful opportunity to create new, cherished memories with your loved ones, while continuing to honor the family traditions that have shaped your life. Just as Paul recognized the sincere faith that was passed down through generations in Timothy's family, you too can leave a lasting legacy of love and tradition.

In this season of life, you have the gift of time—time to invest in your family and to strengthen the bonds that tie you together. Consider starting new traditions that bring joy and meaning to your life and the lives of those you hold dear. Perhaps it's a weekly family dinner, a monthly outing to explore new places, or an annual celebration that brings everyone together.

Let me tell you about Lois, a retired woman who decided to start a new tradition of hosting a yearly family reunion. She would spend months planning activities, meals, and accommodations to ensure that her children, grandchildren, and great-grandchildren could all come together to celebrate their family history and create new memories. These reunions became the highlight of the year, a time for laughter, storytelling, and strengthening family bonds.

Just like Lois, you have the power to create traditions that will be cherished for generations to come. Embrace this opportunity to leave a legacy of love and faith, knowing that the memories you create today will be the stories your family tells tomorrow.

Next Steps

Take a moment to reflect on the traditions that have been meaningful to you and your family. Consider how you can adapt or create new traditions that celebrate your family's unique story. Reach out to your loved ones and involve them in the planning process, fostering a sense of togetherness and shared purpose.

Prayer

Dear God, Thank you for the gift of family and the opportunity to create lasting memories. Guide me as I seek to establish new traditions that honor You and bring joy to those I love. Amen.

22

NAVIGATING FAMILY DYNAMICS

___ / ___ / _____

"If it is possible, as far as it depends on you, live at peace with everyone."

— ROMANS 12:18

amily dynamics can be complex and challenging, especially when interactions with family members may become more frequent. Romans 12:18 encourages us to live at peace with everyone, reminding us of the importance of striving for harmony in our relationships.

Consider the story of Yvonne, who was looking forward to spending more time with her family, especially her two grown children and their families. However, she soon found herself caught in the middle of a conflict between her son and daughter. Their disagreements and misunderstandings created tension at family gatherings, leaving Yvonne feeling stressed and helpless.

Yvonne realized that she needed to find a way to navigate these family dynamics and help resolve the conflicts. She started by reaching out to each of her children individually, listening to their concerns without taking sides. By offering a compassionate ear and encouraging open communication, she helped them understand each other's perspectives.

Yvonne also suggested they seek professional counseling to work through their issues. Her children were initially hesitant, but with gentle encouragement, they agreed. The counseling sessions provided a safe space for them to express their feelings and work towards resolution. Over time, their relationship improved, and family gatherings became more peaceful and enjoyable.

Through this experience, Yvonne learned the value of patience, empathy, and the importance of seeking outside help when needed. Her proactive approach not only helped mend her children's relationship but also strengthened the overall family bond.

Dear reader, navigating family dynamics and handling conflicts can be challenging, but it is essential for maintaining harmony and peace. By approaching conflicts with empathy, patience, and a willingness to seek help, you can foster healthier and more loving relationships within your family.

Next Steps

This week, if you find yourself in the middle of a family conflict, take time to listen to each person's perspective without judgment. Encourage open communication and consider suggesting professional help if needed. Reflect on how your approach can contribute to resolving the conflict and improving family dynamics.

Prayer

Dear God, grant me the wisdom and patience to navigate family conflicts with grace. Help me to be a peacemaker and foster harmony within my family. Amen.

23

OLD FRIENDS, NEW MEMORIES

___ / ___ / _____

"A sweet friendship refreshes the soul."

— PROVERBS 27:9 (MSG)

There's something incredibly comforting about reconnecting with old friends who have shared your journey through various stages of life. As we enter retirement, these relationships can bring renewed joy and a sense of continuity. Proverbs 27:9 reminds us that a sweet friendship refreshes the soul, highlighting the deep satisfaction that comes from maintaining and nurturing these bonds.

When I retired, I made a conscious decision to reconnect with my old friends. We had all been so busy with our careers and families that our interactions had become sporadic. I reached out to a few close friends from different stages of my life—high school, college, and early career days—and we decided to meet up regularly.

One of our favorite activities became our monthly potluck dinners. Each month, we would rotate hosting duties, and everyone would bring a dish to share. These gatherings were filled with laughter, storytelling, and reminiscing about the good old days. We also made new memories together by trying out new recipes, playing games, and even planning small trips.

One particular trip stands out in my memory. We decided to visit a national park we had always talked about but never found the time to see. The trip was filled with adventure and deepened our bond as we explored new trails and shared our lives in a way we hadn't done in years. The experience reminded me of how important it is to maintain these friendships and continue creating new memories together.

Cherish your old friendships and make an effort to maintain them. These relationships are a source of joy, support, and continuity in your life. Whether it's through regular meet-ups, shared hobbies, or special trips, take the time to reconnect with your old friends and create new memories together.

Next Steps

This week, reach out to an old friend you haven't connected with in a while. Plan a simple get-together, like a coffee date or a walk in the park. Focus on rekindling your friendship and creating new memories together.

Prayer

Dear God, thank You for the gift of enduring friendships. Help me to cherish and maintain these relationships, and bless us with new memories and deeper connections. Amen.

24

NEW CONNECTIONS

___ / ___ / _____

"A friend loves at all times, and a brother is born for a time of adversity."

— PROVERBS 17:17

*R*etirement opens up a world of possibilities, including the chance to forge new friendships and expand your social circles. As you embrace this exciting chapter of your life, remember that God has placed within you the capacity to love, to connect, and to cultivate meaningful relationships.

Making new friends can be both exhilarating and intimidating, but it's an essential part of personal growth and fulfillment. Step out of your comfort zone and explore new opportunities to meet like-minded individuals who share your interests and values. Join a local club, volunteer for a cause you're passionate about, or attend events that align with your hobbies and beliefs.

I once met a remarkable woman named Gretel at a community garden. Recently retired, Gretel had decided to pursue her lifelong passion for gardening and joined the local garden club. Through this shared interest, she formed deep, lasting friendships with people from all walks of life. Together, they not only cultivated beautiful gardens but also supported and encouraged one another through life's ups and downs.

Just like Gretel, you have the power to create new connections that enrich your life and bring you joy. Embrace the opportunity to learn from others, share your own experiences, and build a supportive network of friends who uplift and inspire you.

Remember, a true friend loves at all times, and these new friendships can become the family you choose, standing by your side through both good times and adversity.

Next Steps

Identify one new social opportunity that aligns with your interests, such as joining a club, attending a workshop, or volunteering. Take the first step by reaching out and introducing yourself to someone new. Nurture these budding friendships by being a good listener, showing kindness, and finding ways to support and encourage your new friends.

Prayer

Dear God, thank You for the gift of friendship and the opportunity to forge new connections. Give me the courage to step out of my comfort zone and the wisdom to cultivate relationships that honor You. Amen.

25

SUPPORT SYSTEM

___ / ___ / _____

"Carry each other's burdens, and in this way you will fulfill the law of Christ."

*H*ave you ever felt the need for a strong support system during life's transitions? Building a network of friends is especially important when the familiar routines of work life fade away, leaving space for new connections. Galatians 6:2 reminds us of the importance of carrying each other's burdens, emphasizing the value of a supportive network of friends who can uplift and encourage us.

As you navigate this new chapter, consider the ways you can build and strengthen your network of friends. Start by reconnecting with old friends and reaching out to new ones. Whether it's through joining clubs, participating in community events, or attending church groups, there are many opportunities to meet like-minded individuals who share your interests and values.

Investing time and effort into these relationships can lead to meaningful and lasting connections. Share your experiences, listen to their stories, and offer your support. A true friend not only shares in your joys but also stands by you during challenging times, helping you carry your burdens.

Creating a support system doesn't happen overnight, but each step you take towards building these connections will enrich your life. Invite a neighbor for coffee, join a book club, or volunteer for a cause you're passionate about. These small actions can lead to the formation of deep and supportive friendships.

Remember, a strong support system is reciprocal. Be willing to offer your help and encouragement to others as well. As you invest in your friends, you'll find that they will be there to support you in return, creating a network of care and companionship.

Next Steps

This week, take a proactive step to build your support system. Reach out to someone you'd like to get to know better or reconnect with an old friend. Plan an activity or a simple get-together to start strengthening these bonds.

Prayer

Dear God, help me to build a strong support system of friends. Guide me to connect with others and offer support as we carry each other's burdens. Amen.

26

REDISCOVERING US

___ / ___ / _____

"Above all, love each other deeply, because love covers over a multitude of sins."

— 1 PETER 4:8

*W*hen my husband and I both retired, we suddenly found ourselves with an abundance of time together. Initially, this transition was a bit challenging. We had grown accustomed to our individual routines and the hustle and bustle of daily life. However, we saw this new phase as a chance to reconnect and deepen our relationship.

One day, we decided to take a cooking class together. Neither of us was particularly skilled in the kitchen, but we thought it would be a fun way to spend time together. To our surprise, the experience was transformative. Working side by side, chopping vegetables, and following recipes required cooperation and communication. We laughed at our mistakes, celebrated our successes, and enjoyed the fruits of our labor. The simple act of cooking together became a cherished ritual, allowing us to bond over a shared activity.

We also made it a point to start a weekly *"memory night,"* where we would look through old photo albums and reminisce about our journey together. These evenings brought back fond memories and opened up conversations about our hopes and dreams for the future. We realized how far we had come and how much we still had to look forward to.

One of the most profound changes came from our decision to pray together daily. This practice brought a new depth to our relationship, as we shared our hearts and lifted each other up in prayer. It strengthened our spiritual bond and provided a sense of peace and unity.

Through these intentional efforts, we discovered a renewed sense of intimacy and connection. Our retirement years became a season of rediscovery, where we learned to appreciate each other in new ways. The time we invested in our relationship paid off, as we felt closer and more in love than ever before.

Next Steps

This week, choose a new activity to try with your spouse, such as taking a class together or starting a new hobby. Focus on enjoying the time together and building your connection.

Prayer

Dear God, thank You for the gift of my spouse. Help us to deepen our love and strengthen our relationship as we navigate this new season together. Amen.

LIGHT THE PATH FOR ANOTHER
WOMAN

"Give, and it will be given to you. A good measure, pressed down, shaken together and running over, will be poured into your lap."

— LUKE 6:38

Retirement is a beautiful journey, and I hope *"The One-Year Retirement Devotional for Women"* has been a source of purpose, fulfillment, and joy for you. As you continue to explore these devotions, I have a special request.

Would you help someone you've never met, even if you never got credit for it?

Who is this person you ask? They are like you. Or, at least, like you used to be. Less experienced, wanting to make a difference, and needing help, but not sure where to look.

Our mission is to make finding purpose, fulfillment, and joy in retirement accessible to everyone. Everything I do stems from that mission. And, the only way for me to accomplish that mission is by reaching... well...everyone.

This is where you come in. Most people do, in fact, judge a book by its cover (and its reviews). So here's my ask on behalf of a struggling retiree you've never met:

Please help that retiree by leaving this book a review.

Your gift costs no money and less than 60 seconds to make real, but can change a fellow retiree's life forever. Your review could help...

...one more woman find new purpose. ...one more retiree embrace their fulfillment. ...one more reader experience joy in their daily life. ...one more person build meaningful connections. ...one more journey to a peaceful and fulfilling retirement.

To get that 'feel good' feeling and help this person for real, all you have to do is...and it takes less than 60 seconds... leave a review.

Simply scan the QR code below to leave your review:

If you feel good about helping a faceless retiree, you are my kind of person. Welcome to the club. You're one of us.

I'm that much more excited to help you achieve purpose, fulfillment, and joy in your retirement journey faster and easier than you can possibly imagine. You'll love the insights and reflections I've shared in the coming pages.

Thank you from the bottom of my heart. Now, back to our regularly scheduled programming.

• Your biggest fan, Biblical Teachings

P.S. - Fun fact: If you provide something of value to another person, it makes you more valuable to them. If you'd like goodwill straight from another retiree - and you believe this book will help them - send this book their way.

27
TOGETHERNESS

___ / ___ / _____

"Be completely humble and gentle; be patient, bearing with one another in love."

— EPHESIANS 4:2

*D*id you know that the average American couple spends only 35 minutes per day engaging in meaningful conversation? One of the most significant changes you may face in retirement is the increase in time spent with your spouse or loved ones. This newfound togetherness can be a wonderful blessing, but it can also present unique challenges as you navigate uncharted waters.

As you set off on this journey, remember that God has called us to love one another with patience, humility, and gentleness. Embracing this new season with an open heart and a willingness to grow together can lead to a deeper, more fulfilling relationship.

As you contemplate your own journey, it may be helpful to draw inspiration from the story of Mark and Lisa, a retired couple who discovered new depths to their relationship. They realized that their increased time together required a new approach to their relationship. With love and determination, they began to explore new hobbies, both together and separately. They made a point to have regular, open conversations about their needs and desires, and they committed to practicing patience and understanding with one another. Through their efforts, they discovered a renewed sense of joy and appreciation for their life together.

Your journey may look different from Mark and Lisa's, but the principles of love, communication, and patience remain the same. Take this opportunity to rediscover one another, to learn and grow together, and to create new, cherished memories.

Remember, as you navigate this new chapter, keep Christ at the center of your relationship. Let His love guide you, strengthen you, and fill your hearts with joy.

Next Steps

Set aside time this week for a heartfelt conversation with your spouse or loved one. Share your hopes, fears, and expectations for this new season of life. Together, brainstorm ways to nurture your relationship, maintain individual identities, and find joy in your increased time together. Commit to practicing patience, kindness, and understanding as you navigate this new chapter hand in hand.

Prayer

Dear God, Thank you for the gift of my spouse and the opportunity to grow together in this new season. Help us to navigate our increased time together with patience, love, and understanding. Amen.

2 8

COMMUNICATING WITH LOVE

___ / ___ / _____

"Let your conversation be always full of grace, seasoned with salt, so that you may know how to answer everyone."

— COLOSSIANS 4:6

*D*o you believe your communication with loved ones is as good as it could be? It's easy to fall into patterns of complacency, but there's always room to improve how we connect with those we care about. Colossians 4:6 encourages us to let our conversation be full of grace and seasoned with salt, reminding us to speak with kindness and wisdom.

Retirement provides a unique opportunity to enhance your communication skills and deepen your connections with those around you. Start by being an active listener. This means giving your full attention to the person speaking, acknowledging their feelings, and responding thoughtfully. Listening with empathy can bridge gaps and create a sense of understanding and closeness.

It's also important to express yourself clearly and respectfully. Share your thoughts and feelings honestly, but do so with love and consideration for the other person's perspective. Use *"I"* statements to communicate your experiences without placing blame. For example, saying *"I feel concerned when..."* rather than *"You never..."* helps keep the conversation constructive and positive.

Consider the example of a retired couple I know. They found that their communication had become strained after years of busy schedules and limited time together. To address this, they made a conscious effort to improve how they spoke and listened to each other. They scheduled regular *"heart-to-heart"* sessions where they would sit down without distractions and talk openly about their feelings, hopes, and concerns.

These sessions transformed their relationship. They learned to appreciate each other's viewpoints, resolve conflicts more effectively, and support each other's needs. Their conversations became more meaningful and nurturing, strengthening their bond and bringing them closer together.

Next Steps

This week, practice active listening in your conversations. Focus on the speaker without interrupting, and reflect back what you've heard to ensure understanding. Also, make an effort to express your thoughts and feelings using "I" statements to keep the dialogue positive and constructive.

Prayer

Dear God, help me to communicate with love and grace. Guide my words and actions to build stronger, more compassionate relationships with those around me. Amen.

2 9

CELEBRATING MILESTONES

___ / ___ / _____

"Two are better than one, because they have a good return for
their labor: If either of them falls down, one can help the
other up."

— ECCLESIASTES 4:9-10

*H*ave you ever reflected on the journey you and your partner have shared, celebrating the milestones and achievements you've reached together? Retirement offers a wonderful opportunity to cherish these moments and create new memories. Ecclesiastes 4:9-10 reminds us that two are better than one, for they can help each other succeed and lift each other up.

Think about the significant milestones you've achieved as a couple—anniversaries, raising children, career accomplishments, and personal growth. Each of these moments is a testament to the strength and dedication of your partnership. Celebrating these achievements can bring a renewed sense of appreciation and joy into your relationship.

When Jack and Mary retired, they decided to commemorate their 40th wedding anniversary in a special way. They planned a trip to the place where they had honeymooned, revisiting old memories and creating new ones. During the trip, they took time each day to reflect on their journey together, sharing their favorite memories and expressing gratitude for each other.

This celebration was more than just a vacation; it was a reaffirmation of their commitment and love. Jack and Mary returned home with a deeper appreciation for their partnership and a renewed sense of excitement for the years ahead. They realized that celebrating milestones together strengthened their bond and reminded them of the blessings they had experienced.

Just like Jack and Mary, you can find meaningful ways to celebrate the milestones in your partnership. Whether it's a special trip, a simple dinner, or even creating a scrapbook of shared memories, these celebrations can deepen your connection and bring joy to your relationship.

Take time to honor the milestones you've reached with your partner. Celebrate your achievements together and create new memories that will enrich your lives. Remember, two are better than one, and together, you can continue to support and uplift each other.

Next Steps

This week, plan a special activity or event to celebrate a milestone in your partnership. Reflect on your journey together and express gratitude for the achievements and memories you've shared. Notice how this celebration strengthens your bond and brings joy to your relationship.

Prayer

Dear God, thank You for the journey and milestones my partner and I have shared. Help us to celebrate our achievements and continue to support and uplift each other. Amen.

Personal Growth
& Spirituality

30

QUIET TIME

___ / ___ / _____

"Be still, and know that I am God."

— PSALM 46:10

*D*o you find it challenging to carve out quiet moments in your day? In our busy lives, it can be difficult to find time for stillness and reflection. Yet, Psalm 46:10 calls us to "Be still, and know that I am God," reminding us of the profound peace and wisdom that come from spending time in God's presence.

Consider setting aside a specific time each day for prayer and meditation. It might be early in the morning before the house awakens, or in the evening as the day winds down. Find a quiet, comfortable space where you can be alone with your thoughts and prayers. Begin by calming your mind and focusing on your breathing, allowing the stress and distractions of the day to fade away.

Start your quiet time with a simple prayer, inviting God into your heart and asking for His guidance and peace. You might use a favorite scripture verse as a focal point for your meditation, reflecting on its meaning and how it applies to your life. As you meditate, listen for God's voice, allowing His presence to fill you with calm and clarity.

During this time, you can also keep a prayer journal. Write down your thoughts, prayers, and any insights you receive. This practice can help you stay focused and provide a record of your spiritual journey, allowing you to look back and see how God has been working in your life.

Daily prayer and meditation can transform your spiritual life, bringing a deeper sense of peace, purpose, and connection with God. It's a time to rest in His presence, to seek His wisdom, and to renew your spirit.

Dear reader, as you embrace retirement, make daily prayer and meditation a priority. Let these quiet moments with God become a cherished part of your routine, nourishing your soul and strengthening your faith.

Next Steps

This week, commit to setting aside a specific time each day for quiet prayer and meditation. Find a peaceful spot, use a scripture verse for reflection, and keep a journal to track your thoughts and prayers.

Prayer

Dear God, help me to find quiet moments each day to be still and know You. Guide my heart in prayer and meditation, and fill me with Your peace and wisdom. Amen.

3 1

WORDS OF WISDOM

___ / ___ / _____

"Your word is a lamp for my feet, a light on my path."

— PSALM 119:105

*I*n the journey of retirement, there lies a unique opportunity to delve deeper into the wisdom of the Bible. Psalm 119:105 beautifully captures the essence of scripture, describing it as a lamp for our feet and a light on our path, guiding us through life's transitions and challenges.

My friend Amanda found solace and inspiration in Bible study and reflection. With more time on her hands, she decided to join a local Bible study group. This group not only provided her with a structured way to explore the scriptures but also offered a sense of community and support.

Amanda dedicated specific times each day to read the Bible and reflect on its teachings. She kept a journal where she wrote down her thoughts, prayers, and insights from her readings. This practice allowed her to see how God's word applied to her life and to track her spiritual growth over time.

One particular passage that resonated with Amanda was Philippians 4:6-7, which talks about presenting our requests to God and experiencing His peace. Reflecting on this verse helped Amanda navigate the anxieties and uncertainties of retirement. She found that meditating on God's promises brought her comfort and renewed faith.

Amanda's story illustrates the profound impact that regular Bible study and reflection can have on one's spiritual journey. By immersing herself in God's word, she gained wisdom, peace, and a deeper understanding of her purpose in this new season of life.

As you travel the path of retirement, consider dedicating time to Bible study and reflection. Allow the scriptures to be a source of guidance and encouragement, illuminating your path and strengthening your faith.

Next Steps

This week, set aside a specific time each day for Bible study and reflection. Choose a passage to read and reflect on its meaning. Write down your thoughts and prayers in a journal to track your spiritual journey.

Prayer

Dear God, thank You for the wisdom found in Your word. Help me to dedicate time to study and reflect on the Bible, allowing it to guide and strengthen me. Amen.

3 2

FAITH COMMUNITY

___ / ___ / _____

"For where two or three gather in my name, there am I with them."

— MATTHEW 18:20

*D*o you ever feel the need for deeper connections within your faith community? Finding a spiritual family can provide support, encouragement, and a sense of belonging. Matthew 18:20 reminds us that where two or three gather in Jesus' name, He is present with them.

When I retired, I sought to deepen my involvement in my faith community. Attending church services was just the beginning. I joined a small group Bible study where I could share my experiences and learn from others. This group became my spiritual family, offering support and wisdom during both joyful and challenging times.

Volunteering within the church was another way I found connection. Helping with church events, participating in outreach programs, and serving on committees allowed me to use my gifts to benefit others while forming meaningful relationships.

Participating in church activities, such as prayer meetings, worship nights, and fellowship gatherings, also enriched my spiritual life. These events provided opportunities to grow in faith and build lasting friendships with fellow believers.

Finding a spiritual family has brought immense joy and a sense of purpose to my retirement years. It has reminded me of the importance of community in our walk with God.

As you navigate retirement, consider how you can deepen your connections within your faith community. Seek out groups, activities, and volunteer opportunities that resonate with you, and embrace the support and fellowship that comes from being part of a spiritual family.

Next Steps

This week, find a way to engage more deeply with your faith community. Join a small group, volunteer for a church event, or attend a fellowship gathering. Reflect on how these connections enhance your spiritual journey.

Prayer

Dear God, help me to find my spiritual family and deepen my connections within my faith community. Guide me to opportunities where I can grow in faith and fellowship. Amen.

33
NEW HORIZONS

___ / ___ / _____

For I know the plans I have for you," declares the Lord, "plans to prosper you and not to harm you, plans to give you hope and a future."

— JEREMIAH 29:11

 o you ever wonder what new opportunities await you in this season of life? Now is the perfect time to explore new horizons and set personal goals that bring fulfillment and joy. Jeremiah 29:11 reminds us that God has plans for us—plans to prosper us and give us hope and a future.

As you embark on this new chapter, take some time to reflect on your passions and interests. What have you always wanted to do but never had the time for? Whether it's learning a new skill, traveling to new places, or dedicating time to a hobby, setting personal goals can give you a sense of purpose and direction.

Start by writing down a list of things you would like to achieve. Break these goals into smaller, manageable steps, and set realistic timelines for each one. For instance, if you've always wanted to learn to play an instrument, your first step might be to research local music classes or find an online tutorial. If you dream of traveling, begin by planning a small trip and gradually work towards more ambitious journeys.

Consider sharing your goals with a friend or family member who can offer support and encouragement. Having someone to share your progress with can be motivating and help you stay committed. Celebrate each milestone you reach, no matter how small, and give thanks to God for the strength and perseverance He provides.

Setting personal goals not only enriches your life but also helps you grow spiritually and emotionally. It's an opportunity to discover new talents, make meaningful contributions, and live out the plans God has for you.

Next Steps

This week, take time to write down your personal goals. Break them into smaller steps and set timelines for each one. Share your goals with a trusted friend or family member for support and encouragement.

Prayer

Dear God, guide me as I set new personal goals. Help me to pursue these goals with passion and perseverance, trusting in Your plans for my future. Amen.

34

CONTINUOUS GROWTH

___ / ___ / _____

"Let the wise hear and increase in learning, and the one who understands obtain guidance."

— PROVERBS 1:5 (ESV)

*R*etirement marks not an end but a new beginning, a chance to explore and learn in ways you never had time for before. Proverbs 1:5 encourages us to continue growing in wisdom and understanding, highlighting the importance of lifelong learning.

Sarah saw her retirement as an opportunity to embrace new challenges and expand her horizons. Eager to keep her mind active and engaged, Sarah enrolled in various courses at her local community college. From history to art, she explored subjects she had always been curious about but never had the time to study.

Sarah also joined a book club and a writing workshop, where she discovered a passion for literature and creative writing. These activities not only enriched her knowledge but also connected her with a community of like-minded individuals who shared her love for learning. Through these interactions, Sarah found inspiration and motivation to continue pursuing her interests.

One of Sarah's most rewarding experiences was learning to play the piano. She had always dreamed of playing an instrument, and with dedicated practice, she was able to bring beautiful music into her home. This new skill brought her immense joy and a sense of accomplishment, reminding her that it's never too late to learn something new.

This journey illustrates that lifelong learning keeps the mind sharp, the spirit young, and life fulfilling. By continually seeking new knowledge and skills, Sarah found purpose and excitement in her retirement years.

Dear reader, pursue your passions, explore new subjects, and never stop learning. God has blessed you with the ability to grow and adapt, so make the most of this gift and enrich your life through lifelong learning.

Next Steps

This week, identify an area of interest or a skill you've always wanted to learn. Enroll in a course, join a club, or start a new hobby that challenges and excites you. Embrace the joy of continuous growth and discovery.

Prayer

Dear God, help me to embrace lifelong learning and continually grow in wisdom and understanding. Guide me in my pursuits and bless my efforts to enrich my mind and spirit. Amen.

35

DAILY PURPOSE

___ / ___ / _____

"Commit to the Lord whatever you do, and he will establish your plans."

— PROVERBS 16:3

*H*ave you ever wondered how to find a sense of purpose and meaning in your daily life, especially after the routine of work is gone? Retirement offers a wonderful opportunity to rediscover your purpose and find joy in everyday moments. Proverbs 16:3 reassures us that when we commit our actions to the Lord, He will guide our plans and give our days meaning.

When I first entered retirement, I struggled with finding a new sense of purpose. Without the daily demands of a job, I felt a bit adrift. Like I was just waiting to pass over to the next life. However, I soon realized that this new chapter was a chance to redefine my purpose and find meaning in different ways. Here are some practices that helped me, and they might help you too:

1. **Service:** Dedicating time to help others brought immense satisfaction. Volunteering at a local food bank, helping a

neighbor, or offering a listening ear to a friend can add purpose to your days.

2. **Spiritual Growth:** Setting aside time each day for prayer, Bible study, and meditation brought peace and direction. Connecting with God daily can align your actions with His purpose.

3. **Creativity:** Exploring creative outlets like painting, writing, or crafting brought joy and fulfillment. Engaging in creative activities allows you to express yourself and discover new talents.

4. **Relationships:** Strengthening relationships through regular calls, visits, or letters reminded me of the importance of being present for others. These interactions brought joy and a deeper sense of connection.

5. **Gratitude:** Starting each day by listing three things I was grateful for transformed my approach to daily tasks. This practice uplifted my spirit and motivated me to pursue my goals with enthusiasm.

6. **Lifelong Learning:** Engaging in lifelong learning kept my mind active. Whether it's signing up for online courses, attending workshops, or joining discussion groups, learning new things keeps you curious and excited.

As you step into this season of retirement, seek out what gives your days meaning and purpose. Allow yourself time to find them, and when you do? Make sure to keep on filling your life with these types of activities!

Next Steps

This week, choose one of the above practices and incorporate it into your daily routine. Reflect on how this activity adds meaning to your day and aligns with God's purpose for you.

Prayer

Dear God, help me find purpose and meaning in each day. Guide my actions and fill my days with activities that honor You and bring joy to my heart. Amen.

36
ACTIVE LIFE

___ / ___ / _____

*"Do you not know that your bodies are temples of the Holy
Spirit, who is in you, whom you have received from God?
You are not your own."*

— 1 CORINTHIANS 6:19

*D*o you sometimes struggle to stay active in your daily routine? Embracing physical activity is essential for maintaining health and vitality, especially during retirement. 1 Corinthians 6:19 reminds us that our bodies are temples of the Holy Spirit, encouraging us to honor God by taking care of our physical well-being.

Incorporating physical activity into your life doesn't have to be daunting. Start by finding activities that you enjoy and that fit your lifestyle. Whether it's walking, swimming, dancing, or yoga, choose exercises that make you feel good and keep you motivated. The key is to make physical activity a regular part of your routine.

One way to stay committed is to set specific, achievable goals. For example, aim to walk for 30 minutes a day, three times a week, or try a new fitness class at your local community center. Tracking your progress can also be motivating, allowing you to see how far you've come and celebrate your achievements.

Consider joining a group or finding a workout buddy to keep you accountable and make exercising more enjoyable. Social connections can provide encouragement and make physical activity feel less like a chore and more like a fun, shared experience.

Physical activity is not just about exercise; it's about embracing a lifestyle that promotes overall wellness. Pay attention to your body's needs, ensuring you get enough rest, nutrition, and hydration. Listen to your body and adjust your activities as needed to avoid injury and stay healthy.

Next Steps

This week, choose a physical activity that you enjoy and commit to doing it regularly. Set specific, achievable goals and track your progress. Consider inviting a friend to join you for added motivation and support.

Prayer

Dear God, help me to embrace physical activity and take care of my body. Give me the strength and motivation to stay active, honoring You through my commitment to a healthy lifestyle. Amen.

3 7

NOURISHING BODY AND SOUL

___ / ___ / _____

"So whether you eat or drink or whatever you do, do it all for the glory of God."

— 1 CORINTHIANS 10:31

How often do you consider the impact of your diet on both your physical and spiritual well-being? Embracing healthy eating habits is a vital part of caring for the body God has given us. 1 Corinthians 10:31 reminds us to do everything for the glory of God, including the way we nourish our bodies.

I knew a woman named Grace who drastically transformed her eating habits after retirement. Grace had always enjoyed cooking but realized she often chose convenience over nutrition. Determined to improve her health, she began to explore healthy eating and discovered the profound impact it had on her body and soul.

Grace started by incorporating more fresh fruits and vegetables into her meals. She experimented with new recipes that were both nutritious and delicious. By planning her meals and choosing whole foods over processed ones, she noticed an increase in her energy levels and overall well-being.

In addition to physical benefits, Grace found that her mealtime became a time of reflection and gratitude. She began to pray over her meals, thanking God for the nourishment and asking for guidance to make healthy choices. This practice deepened her spiritual connection and made her more mindful of how her food choices honored God.

Grace also shared her journey with friends and family, encouraging them to join her in adopting healthier eating habits. Together, they exchanged recipes, cooked meals, and supported each other in their wellness journeys. This community aspect not only reinforced her commitment to healthy eating but also strengthened her relationships.

Grace's experience shows us that nourishing your body with healthy foods can lead to a more vibrant and fulfilling life. It's a way to honor God by taking care of the temple He has entrusted to you and to enhance your physical and spiritual well-being.

Reflect on your own diet. Does it honor your temple? Are there small ways you could look to improve it?

Next Steps

This week, focus on incorporating more whole foods into your diet. Plan your meals to include a variety of fruits, vegetables, lean proteins, and whole grains. Take time to pray over your meals, expressing gratitude and seeking guidance for healthy choices.

Prayer

Dear God, help me to nourish my body and soul with healthy eating. Guide my choices and bless my efforts to honor You through the way I care for myself. Amen.

38

MIND MATTERS

___ / ___ / _____

"Do not be anxious about anything, but in every situation, by prayer and petition, with thanksgiving, present your requests to God."

— PHILIPPIANS 4:6

*H*ave you ever found yourself feeling overwhelmed or anxious, even during what should be a relaxing time of life? Maintaining mental wellness is crucial, especially in retirement, when life's changes can sometimes feel overwhelming. Philippians 4:6 reminds us not to be anxious, but to bring our concerns to God in prayer, trusting Him to provide peace and guidance.

When I first retired, I expected to feel nothing but joy and relief. Instead, I often found myself feeling restless and anxious. Without the structure and social interactions of my job, I felt a bit lost. Recognizing that I needed to take steps to maintain my mental wellness, I began exploring various practices to help me manage stress and stay mentally healthy.

One of the most impactful changes I made was incorporating daily prayer and meditation into my routine. Each morning, I set aside time to sit quietly, focus on my breathing, and pray. This time of stillness helped me start my day with a sense of calm and centeredness, bringing my worries and hopes to God and feeling His presence in my life.

I also started journaling, which became a therapeutic outlet for my thoughts and emotions. Writing down my feelings allowed me to process them more clearly and recognize patterns that needed attention. It also provided a record of my prayers and reflections, which I could look back on to see how God was working in my life.

Staying socially active was another key to maintaining my mental wellness. I joined a local book club and a community gardening group, both of which provided me with regular social interactions and a sense of purpose. These activities not only kept my mind engaged but also enriched my life with new friendships and shared experiences.

Physical activity also played a vital role in my mental health. I started walking every day, enjoying the fresh air and the beauty of nature. Exercise proved to be a powerful tool for reducing stress and improving my mood.

Through these practices, I learned that maintaining mental wellness requires a holistic approach, integrating spiritual, emotional, and physical care. By prioritizing my mental health, I found a greater sense of peace, purpose, and joy in my retirement years.

Give some of these go, you might surprise yourself at how much better you feel!

Next Steps

This week, choose one new practice to support your mental wellness, such as daily prayer, journaling, joining a social group, or incorporating regular exercise. Reflect on how this practice helps you feel more balanced and peaceful.

Prayer

Dear God, guide me as I seek to maintain my mental wellness. Help me to embrace practices that bring peace and clarity, and fill me with Your calming presence. Amen.

39

HOLISTIC HEALTH

___ / ___ / _____

"Beloved, I pray that all may go well with you and that you
may be in good health, as it goes well with your soul."

— 3 JOHN 1:2 (ESV)

*I*magine waking up each day feeling balanced and energized, knowing that you are caring for your body, mind, and soul in harmony. Achieving a balanced, healthy lifestyle that nurtures both body and soul is essential for overall well-being. 3 John 1:2 encourages us to be in good health and prosper in all aspects of our lives, reflecting the harmony between physical well-being and spiritual health.

Start by considering the different dimensions of wellness: physical, emotional, spiritual, and social. Each of these areas contributes to your overall health and requires attention and care.

- **Physical Wellness:** Embrace activities that keep your body strong and energetic. Regular exercise, a balanced diet, and adequate rest are foundational. Try incorporating a mix of cardio, strength training, and flexibility exercises into your routine. Pay attention to your diet, choosing nutritious foods that fuel your body and support your health.

- **Emotional Wellness:** Take time to nurture your emotional well-being. Practice mindfulness or meditation to reduce stress and enhance your emotional resilience. Journaling can be a powerful tool to process emotions and reflect on your experiences. Seek out activities that bring you joy and fulfillment, and don't hesitate to reach out for support when needed.
- **Spiritual Wellness:** Strengthen your spiritual health through regular prayer, meditation, and study of the scriptures. Engage in practices that bring you closer to God and help you find purpose and meaning. Attend worship services, join a Bible study group, or set aside quiet time each day for personal reflection and connection with God.
- **Social Wellness:** Foster strong, supportive relationships with family, friends, and your community. Building a network of positive, loving connections can enhance your emotional and physical health. Volunteer, participate in group activities, or simply spend quality time with loved ones to nurture these important bonds.

Imagine starting your mornings with yoga to invigorate your body, followed by a quiet time of prayer and meditation to center your spirit. You might join a local community center where you can participate in social events and volunteer opportunities, enriching your social life. Paying close attention to your diet by incorporating fresh, whole foods can also support your overall well-being.

Your commitment to integrating wellness practices can transform your retirement years into a period of vibrant health and spiritual growth. A holistic approach allows you to thrive physically, emotionally, spiritually, and socially.

As you navigate your retirement, consider how you can integrate wellness practices into your life. By nurturing all dimensions of your health, you can achieve a balanced, fulfilling lifestyle that honors God and enhances your well-being.

Next Steps

This week, choose one wellness practice from each dimension—physical, emotional, spiritual, and social—and integrate them into your daily routine. Reflect on how these practices contribute to your overall sense of well-being.

Prayer

Dear God, guide me in integrating wellness practices into my life. Help me to nurture my body, mind, and spirit, achieving holistic health that honors You. Amen.

Enjoying the Retirement Lifestyle

40

WANDERLUST

___ / ___ / _____

"The Lord will watch over your coming and going both now
and forevermore."

— PSALM 121:8

*H*ave you ever felt the excitement of planning a new
adventure? Retirement gave me the perfect opportunity to
embrace my wanderlust and explore the world. Psalm 121:8 reassures me
that the Lord watches over my coming and going, giving me confidence
and peace as I embark on new journeys.

When I first retired, I realized I finally had the time to visit the places I
had always dreamed of seeing. One particular trip that stands out in my
memory is my visit to Italy. I had always been fascinated by its rich
history, stunning landscapes, and delicious cuisine.

Planning the trip was an adventure in itself. I spent hours researching
the best cities to visit, reading about their historical significance, and
planning my itinerary. I discovered charming bed-and-breakfasts,
picturesque walking routes, and must-try local dishes. The more I
planned, the more excited I became.

When I finally arrived in Italy, it was everything I had hoped for and more. I walked through the ancient streets of Rome, marveled at the art in Florence, and enjoyed the serene beauty of the Tuscan countryside. Each day was filled with new experiences and discoveries, deepening my appreciation for God's creation and the diverse cultures of the world.

This journey taught me the importance of being flexible and open to new experiences. Not everything went according to plan, but those unexpected moments often turned into the most memorable ones. I learned to trust in God's guidance, knowing that He was watching over my every step.

Planning adventures has become a source of joy and purpose in my retirement. It allows me to continue learning, growing, and experiencing the beauty of the world. And through it all, I am reminded of God's constant presence and protection.

Next Steps

This week, start planning your next adventure. Make a list of destinations you'd like to visit and begin researching the details. Embrace the excitement of discovering new places and trust in God's protection and guidance as you travel.

Prayer

Dear God, thank You for the opportunity to explore Your beautiful world. Guide me as I plan my adventures and watch over my coming and going. Amen

41

EXPLORING NEW PLACES

___ / ___ / _____

"The earth is the Lord's, and everything in it, the world, and all who live in it."

— PSALM 24:1

*D*id you know that studies show people who travel regularly report higher levels of happiness and life satisfaction? Traveling, whether locally or globally, can be a wonderful way to appreciate the beauty of God's creation and experience His presence in new and diverse ways. Psalm 24:1 reminds us that the earth belongs to the Lord, and exploring it can deepen our connection to Him.

In this season of life, you have the opportunity to explore both local and global destinations more freely. It allows you to experience new cultures, landscapes, and people, enriching your understanding of the world and God's incredible creation.

Think about starting with local travels. There are likely many hidden gems right in your community or nearby towns. Take the time to visit local parks, historical sites, and cultural events. These small adventures can bring a sense of discovery and joy without the need for extensive planning or expense.

On a broader scale, global travel can open your eyes to the vastness and diversity of God's creation. Whether it's a guided tour through the ancient streets of Jerusalem, a serene retreat in the mountains, or a vibrant cultural festival in another country, each experience can deepen your faith and broaden your perspective.

Imagine yourself strolling through a nearby botanical garden, discovering the intricate beauty of each plant and flower. Or picture yourself standing at the foot of the Grand Canyon, marveling at the vastness and majesty of God's handiwork. These experiences, both big and small, can fill your heart with gratitude and awe.

Here are some tips to make the most of your travels:

- **Start Local:** Explore nearby attractions and hidden gems in your community.
- **Plan Ahead:** Research your destinations to make the most of your trips.
- **Stay Open:** Be flexible and open to unexpected experiences and opportunities.
- **Reflect and Share:** Take time to reflect on your travels and share your experiences with others.

By starting locally, you can gradually expand your horizons and build confidence for more extensive travels. Planning ahead helps ensure that you make the most of each trip, while staying open allows you to embrace the unexpected blessings that come your way. Reflecting and sharing your experiences can deepen your appreciation and inspire others to embark on their own journeys.

Traveling is not just about seeing new places; it's about experiencing God's world and finding His presence in every journey. Embrace the adventure with an open heart, and let each trip bring you closer to Him.

Ncxt Steps

This week, plan a visit to a local attraction you haven't explored before. Reflect on how this experience helps you appreciate God's creation and consider planning a more extensive trip in the future.

Prayer

Dear God, thank You for the opportunity to explore Your beautiful world. Guide my travels and help me to see Your hand in every place I visit. Amen.

4 2
MEMORY LANE

___ / ___ / _____

"Remember the wonders he has done, his miracles, and the judgments he pronounced."

— 1 CHRONICLES 16:12

*D*o you ever look back on your travel experiences and feel a rush of joy and gratitude? Capturing travel memories allows us to reflect on the wonders God has shown us and the adventures we have enjoyed. 1 Chronicles 16:12 encourages us to remember the wonders He has done, reminding us of His presence in every journey.

During my travels, each trip was a unique experience filled with learning and growth. But I realized that if I didn't take steps to capture these memories, they might fade with time.

One of my favorite ways to preserve travel memories is through journaling. After each day of exploring, I would take time to write down my thoughts, experiences, and the sights I had seen. This practice not only helped me remember the details but also allowed me to reflect on the spiritual insights I gained during my travels.

Photography became another cherished way to capture memories. I made a habit of taking photos not just of the beautiful landscapes and landmarks but also of the small, meaningful moments—like a friendly conversation with a local or a quiet moment of reflection in a serene spot. These pictures became visual reminders of God's blessings during my travels.

Creating scrapbooks was another enjoyable activity. I collected post-cards, ticket stubs, and small souvenirs from each trip and arranged them alongside my photos and journal entries. These scrapbooks turned into treasured keepsakes that I could share with family and friends, allowing them to experience a piece of my adventures.

Sharing my travel stories with others also became a way to capture and relive those memories. Whether through conversations, writing articles, or giving presentations at my local community center, telling others about my journeys reinforced the experiences in my mind and allowed me to inspire others to explore the world.

Capturing travel memories has enriched my life, providing a lasting record of the wonderful experiences God has blessed me with. It helps me remember His presence in every adventure and keeps the joy of travel alive in my heart. I encourage you to find ways to preserve your own travel memories, so you too can look back and see how God has been with you in every journey.

Next Steps

This week, start a journal or photo album to capture your travel memories. Reflect on your past travels and record your thoughts, experiences, and the spiritual insights you gained. Consider sharing your stories with friends and family to inspire them.

Prayer

Dear God, thank You for the wonderful travel experiences I've had. Help me to capture these memories and remember Your presence in every journey. Amen

43

DOWNTIME BLISS

___ / ___ / _____

*"He makes me lie down in green pastures, he leads me beside
quiet waters, he refreshes my soul."*

— PSALM 23:2-3

*D*id you know that taking regular downtime to relax can
significantly reduce stress and improve your overall well-
being? In our fast-paced world, it's easy to overlook the importance of
relaxation, yet Psalm 23:2-3 reminds us of the refreshment and peace that
comes from resting in God's presence.

As you enjoy the blessings of retirement, you have the wonderful opportunity to embrace moments of relaxation and allow yourself to be
refreshed. This is the perfect time for discovering new ways to unwind
and enjoy the simple pleasures that bring peace to your soul.

Think about the activities that help you feel most at ease. Whether it's
reading a book, taking a leisurely walk, or spending quiet time in prayer
and meditation, these moments of relaxation are essential for maintaining balance and joy in your life.

Imagine yourself sitting in a cozy chair with a favorite book in hand, or perhaps lying in a hammock under the shade of a tree, listening to the gentle rustle of leaves. Picture the tranquility of a serene beach, where the rhythmic sound of waves soothes your spirit. These simple moments of downtime can bring immense peace and happiness.

Here are some ways you can enjoy relaxation:

- **Reading:** Dive into a good book or devotional.
- **Walking:** Take leisurely walks in nature or around your neighborhood.
- **Meditation:** Spend quiet time in prayer or meditation, reflecting on God's word.
- **Listening to Music:** Enjoy soothing melodies or uplifting worship songs.
- **Creative Hobbies:** Engage in activities like knitting, painting, or gardening that bring you joy.

By incorporating these relaxing activities into your daily routine, you can create a rhythm of rest and refreshment. Remember, relaxation is not just about being idle; it's about finding bliss in the moments of quiet and stillness, allowing God to refresh your soul.

Next Steps

This week, choose one relaxing activity to incorporate into your daily routine. Reflect on how this practice helps you feel more peaceful and connected to God's presence.

Prayer

Dear God, thank You for the gift of relaxation. Help me to find bliss in moments of rest and to feel Your refreshing presence in my life. Amen.

44

SERENITY AT HOME

___ / ___ / _____

"Peace I leave with you; my peace I give you. I do not give to
you as the world gives. Do not let your hearts be troubled
and do not be afraid."

— JOHN 14:27

*C*reating a peaceful sanctuary in your home can help you
experience the divine peace that Jesus promises in John 14:27.
This peace transcends worldly troubles and brings tranquility to your
soul.

My sister, Chloe, recently retired and used the time to transform her
home into a haven of tranquility. Chloe realized that after years of a busy
career and raising a family, her home felt cluttered and chaotic. She
longed for a peaceful space where she could relax, reflect, and connect
with God. Chloe started by decluttering her home, removing unneces-
sary items, and keeping only those that brought her joy and peace. This
process not only cleared her physical space but also helped clear her
mind.

Next, Chloe focused on creating calming environments in each room. She added soft lighting, comfortable seating, and soothing colors to her living room, and created a cozy reading nook with a comfortable chair, a soft blanket, and a small table for her Bible and devotional books. In her bedroom, she used light, airy fabrics and added a few plants to bring a touch of nature indoors.

She also dedicated a small corner of her home to prayer and meditation. She placed a comfortable cushion, a small cross, and a candle in this space, making it a dedicated spot for quiet time with God. This simple, intentional space became her refuge, where she could retreat for moments of reflection and prayer.

Chloe's efforts paid off. Her home became a sanctuary of peace and serenity, a place where she felt God's presence more deeply. She discovered that creating a peaceful space at home was a powerful way to nurture her spirit and enhance her sense of well-being. By creating a serene environment, you too can cultivate a space where you feel at peace and connected to God. A peaceful home is a gift you can give yourself, one that provides comfort and spiritual nourishment.

Next Steps

This week, choose one area of your home to declutter and transform into a peaceful space. Add calming elements like soft lighting, comfortable seating, or plants. Dedicate a spot for prayer and reflection.

Prayer

Dear God, help me create a peaceful space in my home where I can feel Your presence and find rest for my soul. Guide me as I transform my surroundings to reflect Your peace. Amen.

45

PEACEFUL PASTIMES

___ / ___ / _____

"Come to me, all you who are weary and burdened, and I will give you rest."

— MATTHEW 11:28

*D*o you ever feel the need to find tranquility and rest in your daily life? Engaging in relaxing activities can bring peace to your mind and body, especially during retirement. Matthew 11:28 invites us to come to Jesus for rest, reminding us that finding moments of calm is essential for our well-being.

There is great importance in incorporating peaceful pastimes into your routine. These activities not only help you to unwind but also provide opportunities for reflection and spiritual growth.

One of my favorite relaxing activities is gardening. Tending to my plants and flowers brings me a sense of calm and fulfillment. The act of nurturing and watching them grow reminds me of God's creation and His care for us. Spending time in my garden allows me to connect with nature and find peace in the beauty around me.

Here are some relaxing activities you might enjoy:

- **Gardening:** Connect with nature and nurture plants.
- **Reading:** Dive into a good book or devotional.
- **Knitting/Crocheting:** Engage in a calming and creative hobby.
- **Walking:** Take leisurely walks in a park or around your neighborhood.
- **Listening to Music:** Enjoy soothing melodies or uplifting worship songs.
- **Drawing/Painting:** Express yourself creatively in a peaceful setting.

Reading has also become a cherished pastime for me. Immersing myself in a good book provides an escape from the busyness of life and offers a chance to learn and reflect. It's a simple yet powerful way to relax and recharge.

Knitting and crocheting have brought me a sense of relaxation and accomplishment. These crafts help to quiet my mind and allow me to create something beautiful. They're wonderful ways to spend time productively while also finding peace.

Engaging in these peaceful pastimes has enriched my retirement, providing moments of calm and helping me maintain a balanced and joyful life. Dear reader, I encourage you to explore relaxing activities that bring you peace and allow you to rest in God's presence.

Nexy Steps

This week, choose one relaxing activity to incorporate into your daily routine. Take time to enjoy this peaceful pastime and reflect on how it brings tranquility and rest to your life.

Prayer

Dear God, thank You for the gift of peaceful pastimes. Help me to find moments of rest and relaxation in my daily life, and draw me closer to You through these activities. Amen.

46
ACKNOWLEDGING
ACHIEVEMENTS

___ / ___ / _____

"Let us not become weary in doing good, for at the proper time
we will reap a harvest if we do not give up."

— GALATIANS 6:9

*H*ave you taken a moment to reflect on how far you've come? Recognizing your progress is crucial for staying motivated and grateful. Galatians 6:9 reminds us that perseverance will lead to a rewarding harvest.

In retirement, you have many milestones to celebrate. These achievements mark your journey and God's faithfulness.

Celebrate personal milestones like anniversaries and birthdays. Each year is a testament to your life's journey and experiences.

Reflect on career achievements. Think about the projects you completed and the challenges you overcame. Your professional impact is a significant part of your story.

Don't forget spiritual milestones. Celebrate your faith growth, deeper prayer life, and service in the church. These are profound and worthy of recognition.

Family milestones are also essential. Cherish the birth of grandchildren, your children's achievements, and family reunions. These moments strengthen bonds and create lasting memories.

Health and wellness milestones matter too. Celebrate steps you've taken to improve your health, like regular exercise and healthy eating. These achievements reflect your commitment to taking care of the body God has given you.

As you acknowledge these milestones, give thanks to God for His guidance. Recognizing your progress brings joy and motivates you to strive for new goals.

Next Steps

This week, reflect on your milestones and write them down. Celebrate these achievements and thank God for His support.

Prayer

Dear God, thank You for guiding me through my journey. Help me to recognize and celebrate my achievements with gratitude and purpose. Amen.

47

HOSTING MEMORABLE EVENTS

___ / ___ / _____

"Offer hospitality to one another without grumbling."

— 1 PETER 4:9

*H*osting memorable events in your home can be a beautiful way to share joy and build community. 1 Peter 4:9 encourages us to offer hospitality to one another without grumbling, highlighting the importance of welcoming others with a generous heart.

Maureen was a woman who discovered joy in hosting gatherings for her family and friends. Maureen had always enjoyed bringing people together, but her busy career had left little time for such activities. Retirement offered her the perfect opportunity to reconnect with her love for hosting.

One summer afternoon, Maureen decided to host a garden party. She spent the week preparing, trimming her garden, planting flowers, and setting up charming seating areas. On the day of the party, Maureen baked her famous lemon bars and arranged a colorful table with her best dishes. The scent of homemade goodies and blooming flowers filled the air, creating an inviting atmosphere.

As her guests arrived, Maureen greeted each one with a warm hug and a genuine smile. The garden quickly filled with lively chatter and laughter. Maureen moved effortlessly among her guests, making sure everyone felt welcomed and included. She introduced new friends to old ones, sparking conversations that flowed naturally.

At one point, Maureen noticed her neighbor, Mrs. Thompson, sitting quietly by herself. Remembering that Mrs. Thompson had recently lost her husband, Maureen gently sat down beside her and engaged her in a heartfelt conversation. By the end of the afternoon, Mrs. Thompson was laughing and sharing stories with the group, her face alight with joy.

The garden party was a resounding success. As the sun set and her guests began to leave, many thanked Maureen for such a wonderful afternoon. She felt a deep sense of fulfillment, knowing that she had created a space for her loved ones to connect and find joy. Her home became a place where people felt comfortable and valued, enriching her retirement years.

Hosting memorable events doesn't have to be elaborate. The key is to focus on making your guests feel special and creating an atmosphere of warmth and welcome. By opening your home and heart to others, you can gather joy and build a community that supports and uplifts each other.

Next Steps

This week, plan a simple gathering at your home. Whether it's a tea party, a potluck dinner, or a game night, focus on creating a warm and welcoming environment for your guests.

Prayer

Dear God, help me to offer hospitality with a generous heart. Guide me as I create joyful gatherings that reflect Your love and bring people together. Amen.

48

MARKING MOMENTS

___ / ___ / _____

"Remember the former things, those of long ago; I am God, and there is no other; I am God, and there is none like me."

— ISAIAH 46:9

*P*ersonal milestones aren't just for the young! Each achievement, no matter how small, becomes an opportunity to reflect on God's blessings and express gratitude. Whether it's a significant birthday, the birth of a grandchild, or the completion of a long-term project, celebrating these moments brings meaning and joy to life.

One personal memorable milestone was the birth of my first grandchild. Holding that tiny life in my arms filled me with immense joy and gratitude. We decided to celebrate this new addition to our family with a special gathering, bringing together loved ones to welcome and pray for the newest member of our family.

Here are some ways you can celebrate personal milestones:

- **Host a Gathering:** Invite loved ones to celebrate with you.

- **Create a Memory Book:** Document your milestones with photos and reflections.
- **Take a Special Trip:** Celebrate by visiting a meaningful destination.
- **Give Thanks:** Spend time in prayer, thanking God for His blessings.
- **Share Your Story:** Inspire others by sharing your journey and achievements.

Marking these moments doesn't have to be elaborate. Even a simple acknowledgment can bring joy and a sense of accomplishment. I found that creating a memory book, filled with photos and reflections, was a wonderful way to commemorate these special times. Each page became a testament to God's grace and the journey He has led me on.

Engaging in these practices has enriched my retirement, providing moments of joy and gratitude. I encourage you to find ways to celebrate your personal milestones, recognizing the seasons of your life and God's presence in each one.

Next Steps

This week, identify a recent personal milestone and choose a way to celebrate it. Reflect on how this milestone marks a season in your life and give thanks for God's blessings.

Prayer

Dear God, thank You for the milestones in my life. Help me to celebrate these moments with joy and gratitude, recognizing Your hand in every achievement. Amen.

49

JOURNALING YOUR JOURNEY

___ / ___ / _____

"I remember the days of long ago; I meditate on all your works
and consider what your hands have done."

— PSALM 143:5

*H*ave you considered the power of reflecting on your year through journaling? Keeping a journal helps you meditate on God's works in your life, as Psalm 143:5 encourages us to do. It's a wonderful way to document your journey and see His hand in every moment.

As you embrace retirement, journaling can be a fulfilling practice. Here are some tips and tricks to help you get started and make the most of your journaling journey:

1. **Set a Regular Time:** Find a consistent time each day or week to write in your journal. Whether it's in the morning with your coffee or in the evening before bed, setting a routine helps make journaling a habit.
2. **Choose the Right Journal:** Pick a journal that feels right for you. It could be a beautifully bound book, a simple notebook, or

even a digital journal. The important thing is that it's something you enjoy using.

3. **Start with Gratitude:** Begin each entry by listing a few things you're grateful for. This practice sets a positive tone and helps you focus on the blessings in your life.

4. **Reflect on Your Day:** Write about the events of your day, your thoughts, and your feelings. Reflect on how you saw God's hand at work and what you learned from your experiences.

5. **Set Goals and Track Progress:** Use your journal to set personal goals and track your progress. This could be anything from health and wellness goals to spiritual growth and new hobbies.

6. **Incorporate Scripture:** Include Bible verses that resonate with you. Reflect on how these scriptures apply to your life and the insights they provide.

7. **Be Honest:** Don't shy away from writing about challenges and struggles. Honesty in your journaling allows for genuine reflection and growth.

8. **Use Prompts:** If you're not sure what to write about, use journaling prompts. Questions like "What did I learn today?" or "How did I see God's presence in my life?" can help spark your writing.

9. **Review and Reflect:** Periodically read back through your journal entries. Reflect on your growth, the lessons learned, and God's faithfulness throughout your journey.

10. **Express Creativity:** Feel free to include drawings, photos, or other creative elements in your journal. It's a personal space for you to express yourself fully.

Journaling is a powerful tool for reflection and spiritual growth. As you document your journey, you'll find that it helps you stay connected to God's presence and recognize His blessings in your life.

Next Steps

This week, start a journal and commit to writing regularly. Use the tips above to guide you and see how reflecting on your journey enhances your sense of gratitude and spiritual growth.

Prayer

Dear God, help me to reflect on my journey through journaling. Guide my thoughts and help me to see Your hand in every moment. Amen.

50
HEART OF GRATITUDE

___ / ___ / _____

"Give thanks in all circumstances; for this is God's will for you in Christ Jesus."

— 1 THESSALONIANS 5:18

*P*racticing gratitude is a powerful way to enhance your sense of well-being and deepen your relationship with God. 1 Thessalonians 5:18 reminds us to give thanks in all circumstances, highlighting the importance of maintaining a heart of gratitude.

Consider the story of my Grandma, whose life was a testament to the power of gratitude. Despite facing numerous challenges, she always found reasons to be thankful. Her practice of appreciation was evident in the small, everyday moments that many might overlook.

Grandma had a tradition of keeping a gratitude journal. Every evening, she would sit by the window with a cup of tea, reflecting on her day and writing down three things she was grateful for. Some entries were simple —like the beauty of a sunset or a kind word from a neighbor—while others were profound, like the strength to overcome a difficult situation.

One particularly challenging year, our family faced numerous trials, including financial difficulties and health issues. Yet, Grandma's gratitude never wavered. I remember one evening when she shared an entry from her journal: "Today, I am grateful for the roof over our heads, the food on our table, and the love we share as a family." Her unwavering gratitude helped us all to see the blessings amidst the struggles.

She also expressed her appreciation through acts of kindness. She would bake cookies for our neighbors, write thank-you notes to friends, and volunteer at the local shelter. These small acts were her way of giving back and showing appreciation for the community that supported her.

Her gratitude was contagious. Inspired by her example, I started my own gratitude journal. This practice transformed my perspective, helping me to focus on the positive aspects of my life and see God's hand in every circumstance.

One of the most memorable lessons in gratitude came during a family reunion. Despite her arthritis, Grandma insisted on preparing a home-made feast for everyone. As we gathered around the table, she led us in a heartfelt prayer of thanks, reminding us of the importance of appreciating each other and the blessings we had.

Through her practice of gratitude, Grandma taught us that appreciating the small things in life leads to a deeper sense of joy and contentment. Her heart of gratitude was a constant reminder of God's goodness and faithfulness.

As you reflect on your own life, consider adopting a practice of gratitude. Whether it's keeping a journal, expressing thanks through kind acts, or simply pausing to appreciate the beauty around you, cultivating a heart of gratitude can transform your perspective and bring you closer to God.

Next Steps

This week, start a gratitude journal. Each day, write down three things you are thankful for. Reflect on how this practice changes your outlook and deepens your appreciation for the blessings in your life.

Prayer

Dear God, thank You for the countless blessings in my life. Help me to cultivate a heart of gratitude and to appreciate Your goodness in all circumstances. Amen.

51

EMBRACING YOUR GROWTH

___ / ___ / _____

*"Consider it pure joy, my brothers and sisters, whenever you
face trials of many kinds, because you know that the
testing of your faith produces perseverance."*

— JAMES 1:2-3

*D*o you ever take time to reflect on the lessons you've learned
throughout your life? Embracing the growth that comes from
our experiences, both good and bad, is essential for personal and spiritual development. James 1:2-3 encourages us to find joy even in our trials,
knowing that they produce perseverance and growth in our faith.

In retirement, I've found it valuable to look back on the lessons life has
taught me. Each challenge and triumph has shaped who I am today.
Reflecting on these experiences has allowed me to see God's hand in my
journey, guiding me through every season.

One significant lesson I've learned is the importance of patience and
trust in God's timing. There were moments in my life when I felt lost or
impatient, wondering why things weren't happening as I had planned.

But looking back, I see how God's timing was perfect, leading me to opportunities and blessings I couldn't have anticipated.

Another lesson is the value of forgiveness, both of others and myself. Holding onto grudges or regrets only weighs us down. By embracing forgiveness, I found peace and the ability to move forward with a lighter heart.

Here are some ways you can embrace your growth:

- **Reflect on Your Experiences:** Take time to journal or meditate on the lessons you've learned.
- **Celebrate Your Progress:** Acknowledge how far you've come and the growth you've experienced.
- **Share Your Wisdom:** Inspire others by sharing the lessons you've learned and how they've shaped you.
- **Seek Continuous Growth:** Stay open to new experiences and lessons that can further your personal and spiritual development.

Reflecting on these lessons has brought me immense gratitude and a deeper understanding of my faith journey. Sharing these insights with others, whether through conversations, writing, or teaching, has allowed me to connect and inspire those around me.

Embracing growth means acknowledging both the joys and the hardships of life, seeing them as opportunities for learning and transformation. It's about recognizing God's presence in every moment and trusting that He is shaping us according to His perfect plan.

As you reflect on your own journey, consider the lessons you've learned and how they've contributed to your growth. Embrace these experiences with gratitude, and let them guide you toward a deeper relationship with God and a richer, more fulfilling life.

Next Steps

This week, take some time to reflect on the significant lessons you've learned throughout your life. Write them down and consider how they have shaped your growth. Share one of these lessons with a friend or loved one.

Prayer

Dear God, thank You for the lessons I've learned and the growth they've brought. Help me to embrace these experiences with gratitude and continue to guide me on my journey. Amen.

52

PLANNING FOR THE FUTURE

___ / ___ / _____

*"For I know the plans I have for you," declares the Lord, "plans
to prosper you and not to harm you, plans to give you hope
and a future."*

— JEREMIAH 29:11

*H*ave you thought about how you want to shape your
future? Jeremiah 29:11 reminds us that God has plans to
give us hope and a future. Embracing this promise, retirement is the
perfect time to envision and plan the next chapter of your life.

As you look forward, consider these tips to help you plan for a fulfilling
future:

1. **Set Clear Goals:** Determine what you want to achieve in the
   coming years. Whether it's traveling, learning new skills, or
   volunteering, setting clear goals gives you direction and
   purpose.
2. **Stay Connected:** Maintain and build relationships with family,
   friends, and your faith community. Strong social connections
   are vital for emotional and spiritual well-being.

3. **Embrace Lifelong Learning:** Keep your mind active by pursuing new interests. Take classes, read books, or join discussion groups to continue growing and learning.

4. **Prioritize Health and Wellness:** Focus on maintaining your physical health through regular exercise, a balanced diet, and routine check-ups. Consider activities like yoga, swimming, or walking to stay active.

5. **Spiritual Growth:** Deepen your relationship with God through prayer, Bible study, and meditation. Join a small group or attend retreats to strengthen your faith.

6. **Financial Planning:** Review your finances and make plans to ensure financial stability. Consult with a financial advisor if needed to manage your resources effectively.

7. **Volunteer and Give Back:** Find ways to serve others in your community. Volunteering can provide a sense of purpose and fulfillment, helping you stay engaged and connected.

8. **Pursue Hobbies and Passions:** Dedicate time to activities you love. Whether it's gardening, painting, or playing music, engaging in hobbies can bring joy and satisfaction.

9. **Travel and Explore:** If travel is one of your goals, start planning your adventures. Whether exploring local attractions or far-off destinations, travel can enrich your life and broaden your perspectives.

10. **Reflect and Adjust:** Regularly review your goals and progress. Be open to adjusting your plans as needed, staying flexible to embrace new opportunities and challenges.

As you move forward into this new chapter of retirement and beyond, remember to seek God's guidance in all your endeavors. Trust in His plans for you and embrace the journey with hope and enthusiasm. This devotional year may be ending, but the journey of growth and discovery continues. Carry forward the lessons, reflections, and goals you have set, knowing that God's guidance and love are with you every step of the way.

Next Steps

This week, take some time to outline your future goals. Pray for God's guidance as you plan, and write down actionable steps to help you achieve these goals.

Prayer

Dear God, thank You for the plans You have for my future. Guide me as I envision and plan the next chapter of my life. Help me to trust in Your guidance and embrace the opportunities ahead. Amen.

PASS ON THE WISDOM

"Therefore encourage one another and build each other up, just as in fact you are doing."

— - 1 THESSALONIANS 5:11

*N*ow that you've completed *"The One-Year Retirement Devotional for Women,"* you have a wealth of knowledge and inspiration to help you find purpose, fulfillment, and joy in retirement. It's time to share your newfound wisdom and show other readers where they can find the same guidance.

Simply by leaving your honest opinion of this book on Amazon, you'll show other retired women where they can find the encouragement and insights they're looking for, helping them discover peace and fulfillment in this new chapter of life.

Thank you for your help. The journey of retirement is enriched when we share our knowledge and experiences with others – and you're helping me to do just that.

SCAN ME

Your review is a testament to your journey and a beacon of hope for other women entering or navigating retirement. By sharing your thoughts, you're supporting the mission of this devotional and encouraging others to find their paths to fulfillment and joy.

Thank you for being a part of this community of women embracing retirement with grace and confidence. May God continue to bless you and use you as a light in the lives of others.

With gratitude,

Biblical Teachings

AND SO, THE JOURNEY
CONTINUES...

As you reach the end of this year-long devotional journey, take a moment to reflect on the growth and changes you've experienced. Each week, you have explored new dimensions of your faith, discovered new purposes, and strengthened your connections with others and with God.

The transition into retirement is not just an end but a new beginning. It's a time to embrace the wisdom you've gained, the relationships you've nurtured, and the spiritual insights you've discovered. Reflect on how these devotions have helped you navigate the challenges and joys of this season of life.

Remember that the journey doesn't end here. Continue to seek God's guidance in every aspect of your life. Let the lessons and habits you've developed over the past year inspire you. Keep finding new ways to serve, love, and connect with those around you.

As you move forward, carry with you the peace and fulfillment that comes from a closer relationship with God. Share your experiences and the joy you've found with others, becoming a beacon of hope and encouragement in your community.

Thank you for allowing this devotional to be a part of your journey. It has been an honor to share these reflections and stories with you. I pray they will continue to inspire, challenge, and draw you closer to God's heart. May you always remember that you are loved, valued, and have a unique purpose in Christ.

Keep moving forward with grace and confidence, knowing God's plans for you are filled with hope and a future. Your best days are ahead, and the most fulfilling chapter of your life is just beginning.

With love and prayers,

The team at Biblical Teachings